Irish
Country Houses

TERENCE REEVES-SMYTH

G000125747

APPLETREE GUIDE

Published and printed by
The Appletree Press Ltd
19–21 Alfred Street
Belfast BT2 8DL
1994

British Library Cataloguing-in-Publication Data
A catalogue record for this book is
available from the British Library.

ISBN 0 86281 373 5

9 8 7 6 5 4 3 2 1

Picture Acknowledgements

Bord Failte: pages 17, 35, 37, 39, 51, 64, 68, 75, 76, 81, 85
The National Trust: pages 7, 25, 26, 29, 31, 41, 45, 47, 66, 95

CONTENTS

1. Ardress	16. Castletown
2. The Argory	17. Kilkenny Castle
3. Huntington Castle	18. Emo Court
4. Mount levers Court	19. Glin Castle
5. Bantry House	20. Springhill
6. Dunkathel	21. Carrigglas Manor
7. Fota Island	22. Beaulieu
8. Muckross House	23. Westport House
9. Castle Ward	24. Clonalis
10. Mount Stewart	25. Strokestown Park
11. Malahide Castle	26. Lissadell
12. Newbridge	27. Lismore Castle
13. Castle Coole	28. Belvedere
14. Florence Court	29. Tullynally Castle
15. Kylemore Abbey	30. Russborough

INTRODUCTION

Once standing at the focus of Irish social and political life, country houses in Ireland remain a splendid surviving testimony to the confidence and rich culture of generations of Ireland's ruling families. For centuries the 'Big House' drew upon the best craftsmanship and artistic skills that Ireland had to offer. Nowhere else can visitors today so fully appreciate the remarkable quality and distinctive character of eighteenth- and nineteenth-century Irish craft, evidenced by its plaster-work, joinery, wrought-iron work and stonework and the artistry of its furniture, pictures, silver, glass, pottery and porcelain. Despite the tragic loss of so many country houses over the past seventy years, enough remains for us to enjoy this unique legacy of Ireland's past.

This book is designed to provide information on country houses that are open to the public on a regular basis, though a handful of important houses open only by appointment has also been added. Every effort has been made to provide a representative selection of houses, though inevitably the choice reflects both a personal taste and the constraints of this book. The central idea has been to include enough background information on the history and contents of each house that visitors will gain some impression of what to expect; more detailed guide books are normally available at each property.

The houses in this book are arranged alphabetically on an all-Ireland county basis. Opening times and other practical details are given at the end of each entry, as well as the National Grid Reference number (NGR). Further information about other country houses open to the public may be obtained from Irish Heritage Properties, 3a Castle Street, Dalkey, County Dublin (01 2859323), or from Bord Failte, Baggot Street Bridge, Dublin 2 by sending a self-addressed envelope and IR £1.50. In Northern Ireland country houses open to the public are confined almost entirely to properties owned by the National Trust: Rowallane, Saintfield, County Down, BT24 7LH. Further information on over 2,000 country houses, many now demolished or in ruins, can be gleaned from Mark Bence-Jones's indispensable *Guide to Irish Country Houses*, published by Constable.

ARDRESS

County Armagh

Irish country houses that have developed over the centuries have always held a special fascination and charm, and none more so than Ardress – a modest gentleman farmer's residence with aspirations of grandeur. Originally a seventeenth-century house, it was enlarged with a hotch-potch of extensions at various times between 1780 and 1810 – all cleverly incorporated behind symmetrically composed façades. One of these additions includes a splendid drawing-room that could belong to a sophisticated Dublin town mansion of the period; above all else it gives Ardress its elegance and distinction.

The central portion of Ardress, behind the five centre windows of the front façade, is a two-storey gable-ended house built sometime around 1670 for the Clarke family. It has a rectangular plan and retains its original steeply pitched butt-purlin roof of local oak – a type of roof-timbering that is only known in five other Ulster houses but is characteristic of vernacular roof carpentry techniques found in many seventeenth-century box-framed houses in England. Internally the house retains its tripartite plan, with a long, narrow hall flanked by the parlour on the left and the former kitchen to the right. In 1700 a new kitchen extension was built to the rear of the house and the present oak staircase erected at one end of the former kitchen, while the remaining area, now known as the inner hall, was integrated with the hall by knocking an arch through the wall. The parlour retains its early proportions and now contains some fine Irish furniture, notably an oak and applewood bureau bookcase made locally circa 1725, a walnut chest dating from 1700 and a good regency-period Pembroke table; the Italian marble scagliola chimney-piece was probably installed around 1740.

A door from the parlour leads into the great surprise of the house – the magnificent drawing-room added in 1780 by the Dublin architect George Ensor, brother of the better-known architect John Ensor. George married the heiress Sarah Clarke in 1760 and decided to settle at Ardress with his wife in 1778 upon his retirement as Clerk of Works to the Surveyor General. The new room was decorated by one of the great stuccodores of the age, Michael Stapleton – the great Irish master of the restrained neo-classical plasterwork associated with Adam. Stapleton's decorative ceiling design at Ardress is among his best works; it comprises intertwining segments of circles embellished by delicate foliage, urn motifs and a central plaque representing Aurora in 'The Chariot of the Dawn'. More classical medallions are arranged symmetrically on the centre of each wall and are festooned with delicate husk chains. The present colour scheme is based on a free interpretation of the pink and green watercolour tints shown in Stapleton's original drawings in the National Library of Ireland. Prior to 1961 the walls were a sharp green with the decorative plasterwork, frieze and ceiling left white. The room's plasterwork is suitably complemented by a pair of neo-classical settees, a pair of gilded *torchères* with sphinx heads and two fine commodes.

The house assumed its present appearance after a series of additions between 1790 and 1810, some of which were evidently made by the author George Ensor (1772–1845) soon after he inherited Ardress from his father in 1803. Two bays of windows were added to each end of the front façade in order to impress – an

The front façade of Ardress

exercise that involved constructing no less than five dummy windows and a partly false front but which allowed the formation of an elegant garden front with curved sweeps at right angles to the main façade. New wings were added to the north and east sides, the latter containing the dining-room which curiously was linked to the drawing-room by a colonnade along the garden front and was later removed in 1879. The room was restored in 1961 and now contains some exceptional furniture, most strikingly a heavily carved grotesque Irish Chippendale side-table and a pair of commodes made in 1759 by Pierre Langlois. Here hangs a fine collection of paintings from Stuart Hall near Stewartstown and now on permanent loan to the National Trust. They include a group of 'Four Seasons' by Theobald Michau, 'The Road to Calvary' by Frans Francken the younger and 'Christ on the Road to Emmaus' signed by J. Myts (1645–64).

Ardress was inherited in 1845 by the third George Ensor who died unmarried in 1879. The property then passed to his nephew Charles Ensor, and later to Charles's son Captain Charles H. Ensor who sold Ardress to the National Trust in 1960. In addition to upgrading the house, the Trust have restored the mainly eighteenth-century farmyard where visitors can inspect a milking shed, dairy, boiler house, forge and threshing barn. There is also an interesting display of old farm implements.

Located 7 miles from Portadown on the Moy Road (B28). NGR: H 914559. Open April, May, June and September: Saturdays, Sundays and bank holidays, 2.00 – 6.00 pm. Open daily during Easter: 2.00 – 6.00 pm. Open daily during July and August, except Tuesdays: 2.00 – 6.00 pm. Farmyard open May, June and September: weekdays except Tuesdays, 12.00 – 4.00 pm. Toilet facilities. Admission to house, grounds and farmyard: adults £2.20; children £1.00; groups £1.60. Admission to grounds and farmyard only: adults £1.60; children £0.75; groups £1.40. Tel: (0762) 851236.

THE ARGORY

County Armagh

There is a touch of the Marie Celeste about the Argory, as if time had stood still a century ago and its occupants might at any moment return from their vanished world, bringing the place to life. The house is neither large nor grand by nineteenth-century standards. Its importance lies in the remarkable survival of its interior which, unique in Ireland, evokes the atmosphere and ambience of late Victorian country-house life.

The Argory was built between 1819 and 1824 by Walter McGeough, alias MacGeough, who assumed the additional name of Bond in 'affectionate regard to the family of his deceased grandmother' upon completion of the house. His decision to build a house here was influenced by his father's will. According to its terms only £400 a year was left to the eldest son William; the bulk of the fortune went to the younger son Walter and his three sisters. Rather curiously, the will stipulated that once Walter married he was no longer allowed to live at Drumsill, the family seat outside Armagh, so long as two of his sisters remained unwed. Although one sister died early, Walter judged correctly that the others would remain husbandless and therefore decided to build his own house on lands he had inherited at Derrycaw, overlooking the River Blackwater.

The commission for the new house went to two young Dublin-based architects, John and Arthur Williamson, almost certainly on the personal recommendation of Francis Johnson who was related to Walter's mother. Surprisingly little is known about the Williamsons, though it is clear from the style of their work at the Argory that they trained in Johnson's office. Most of the original plans and accounts relating to the building were lost in 1898 when a fire broke out in the octagonal pavilion, but it is known that the house was originally designed as a single block with the north wing added later. The Argory has imposing ashlar-faced elevations in a restrained classical style. The centre of its two-storey seven-bay west front breaks forward under a shallow pediment and contains a porch whose doorcase is framed by an elliptical arch and embellished with a squashed fanlight, glazed side panels and a lion's mask. This leads directly into the staircase hall, which once served as the front hall until the 1830s when the main entrance overlooking the river was shifted to the less exposed east side, where a small portico was added.

The staircase hall, or west hall, has been described as one of the most exciting interiors of its date in Ireland. It has a theatrical cantilevered staircase with brass banister supports, marbled walls, colza-oil lamp (converted to gas in 1906) and a large cast-iron stove surmounted by a replica of the Warwick vase. The original 1821 drawings of this stove survive; its flue descends beneath the floor to the drawing-room chimney. The room also has an almost life-size bronze cast of a mastiff, one of two bronzes of dogs which date from 1835 and are early examples of the work of the French *animalier* Charles Fratin.

The decorative scheme of the staircase hall with its marbled walls is continued upstairs in the organ gallery – a broad landing extending through the width of the house with tripartite 'Wyatt windows' at each end. Wilkie prints in ornate gilded frames hang at the staircase end, while at the other stands the very large cabinet barrel organ which is generally accepted as the most important of its kind in existence. This recently restored instrument was commissioned in 1822 from the London organ builder James Bishop; it originally had six barrels, Samuel Wesley being consulted in their selection, but now only three survive.

Perhaps the most attractive of the reception rooms at the Argory is the drawing-room, which lay shrouded in dust-sheets from 1939 until 1979. It was remodelled in the 1890s when the windows were lengthened and a small anteroom and cupboard were run into the room making it larger and brighter. The Carrara marble chimney-piece with baseless Doric columns is original, but most of the furnishing of this comfortable room is late nineteenth century. There are rich curtains and upholstery, copies of old masters in gilt frames on the walls, a Steinway rosewood grand piano bought in 1898 and a workbox nearby ready for use. Other items include two *pietro duro* round tables which came from Drumsill in 1916, one of which is inlaid with butterflies and the other with the quartered coat of arms of MacGeough and Bond. The ormolu colza-lamp was converted to gas in 1906 when an acetylene gas plant was installed in the yard for £257 17s. 6d. – a sum which included all the fittings, such as the wall brackets each side of the overmantel mirror. The Argory has never been lit by electricity, though the National Trust installed carefully concealed power points when they took over the house in 1979.

On the other side of the staircase hall is the dining-room. Much of its furniture was acquired from the Glasgow firm of cabinetmakers and upholsterers James Whyte and Son in 1827, notably the chairs around the long table – which is set with family china and silver for tea. Family portraits line the walls as is so often the case in Irish country house dining-rooms, while some of the accessories in the room include two round-topped tables in mahogany adjusted by a system of internal pulleys and two side-tables, beneath which stand plate buckets and a tea caddy; a warming cabinet sits to the left of the fireplace.

Across the central corridor from the dining-room lies the billiard room – a familiar feature of nineteenth-century country houses, though it is rare to see one so well preserved as this. The room retains its original early nineteenth-century table by Burroughes & Watts as well as its early accessories, such as its scoreboard, level, cue stand and rests. The masculine feel of the room is emphasised by the warm appearance of the dado, which has been painted to resemble panelling, while the shutters have been grained to imitate walnut veneer. The other major reception room, the study, contains more family portraits, including a striking one of Walter McGeough by Sir Frederick Grant. This room, which continued to be regularly used by W. A. N. MacGeough Bond until his recent death, reveals a cluttered and reposeful scene crammed with an assortment of family acquisitions spanning four generations.

The Argory and most of its contents were given to the National Trust by the late W. A. N. MacGeough Bond in April 1979. Two years later the house was opened to the public following a major restoration, which included work to the stable block, designed in 1820 and surmounted by a cupola with an eight-day striking clock and a handsome weather-vane. The 300-acre demesne park has many pleasant walks.

Located 4 miles from Moy on the Derrycaw Road. NGR: H 872580. Open April, May, June and September: Saturdays, Sundays and bank holidays, 2.00 – 6.00 pm. Open daily during Easter: 2.00 – 6.00 pm. Open daily during July and August, except Thursdays: 2.00 – 6.00 pm. Gift shop and tea room open as house. Toilet facilities. Admission: adults £2.20; children £1.00; groups £1.60. Tel: (08687) 84753.

HUNTINGTON CASTLE

County Carlow

The first view of the attractive grey-rendered castle of Huntington leaves one in no doubt that this is a building of great character and antiquity. Approached from the village of Clonegal down a straight seventeenth-century lime avenue, its three-storey four-bay castellated front seems hardly to have a straight line anywhere – the side walls gently leaning to one angle and the sash windows lying askew. Additions, alterations and a mixture of styles accumulated over the centuries add enormously to Huntington's charm, while a treasure trove of varied contents reflects family ownership spanning three and a half centuries.

The old core of Huntington Castle is a tower house built by Laurence, first and last Lord Esmonde, between 1625 and 1630 on the site of a medieval stronghold of the Kavanaghs and latterly of the Nettervilles. A remarkable yew walk nearby possibly belongs to the late seventeenth century, though claims that these trees were planted as early as the fifteenth century cannot be entirely discounted. Other formal garden features, which include a canal and the impressive lime avenue, were created after 1678 when Sir Lawrence Esmonde, second Bart, returned from French exile and transformed the castle from a garrison into a family home. Sash windows were installed in the castle's walls, partitions dividing the various floors were inserted between rooms – along with plaster panelling in the dining-room, drawing-room and four-poster room above – while the porch and a long, low two-storied wing were also added. The lugged door and window architraves, however, and a rather attractive granite chimney-piece with shell centre-piece belong to later improvements made in the 1720s by Sir John Esmonde, third Bart.

The castle remained largely unaltered until 1849 when the property was inherited by Alexander Durdin, whose grand-uncle had married the two daughters and co-heirs of Sir John Esmonde, third Bart, as his two successive wives. In 1860 Alexander Durdin began additions to the rear of the castle facing the yard where there are irregular two-storey battlemented ranges. He also embarked on a disastrous attempt to enlarge the castle's basement windows, causing subsidence in the walls and the collapse of the drawing-room ceiling, which he replaced with a strapwork plaster design whose Elizabethan style fits very comfortably in the room.

Alexander Durdin's modifications to the house were continued by his daughter Helen following her marriage in 1880 to Herbert Robertson – formerly Tory MP for Hackney South. They built the tapestry room and the library above it, completed the wing to the rear with its large bow-ended bedroom, added a chapel with an organ and moved the castle entrance to the west side so that the avenue turned the building around into the yard. Aside from the bathrooms with plumbed water, a great rarity in those days – as well as central heating – electricity was also installed in 1888, power for which was generated from a water turbine on the River Derry. Huntington was one of the first country houses in Ireland to have electricity, and in order to satisfy local interest a light was kept burning on the front lawn so that the curious could come up and inspect it. Subsequent alterations at Huntington were carried out by Helen Robertson's son, Manning Durdin-Robertson, who was himself an architect. He designed the conservatory on the south side of the castle in the early 1890s, including its railings which were originally intended to be of wrought iron but instead were carved by local masons in granite.

With its endless number of passages and flights of stairs on nine different levels, its dark vaulted basements and fifteen-foot holy well, its Temple of Isis drawing followers of Egyptian mythology, and its marvellously atmospheric rooms, Huntington is indeed a house of profound character, filled with the spirits of the past. Among the most memorable rooms are the library, with ten-foot-high bookshelves and a wonderful smell of old leather; the tapestry room below, with striking French nineteenth-century loomed tapestries and an Aubusson carpet from the 1750s brought back from France by an RIC sergeant; and the conservatory, which houses an old vine – a cutting from a plant at Hampton Court dating around 1900. Close by lies the drawing-room, a cheerful area with a finely carved oak chimney-piece dated 1860, a Bechstein piano and a collection of porcelain including a large *famille verte* bowl looted by a soldier from the Imperial Palace in Peking, bought subsequently by Lieutenant General Sir L. W. Parsons and later acquired by his daughter Nora, author of *The Crowned Harp*, who married Manning Robertson in 1912.

Perhaps the most interesting of all rooms is the dining-room, formerly the old hall of the castle. Its granite fireplace has the date 1625 inscribed on the keystone. A steel door masquerading as a fireback reveals a serving hatch for food when opened – essentially a low passage through the thickness of the wall leading into the kitchen. To the right is a stained-glass genealogical window made in 1870 by Powell which traces the family's lineage back to Lord Esmonde, while the medieval atmosphere of the room is further enhanced by Bedouin tent hangings from Tunisia draped across the walls. The great double doors leading into the adjacent front porch have spy-holes and musket holes – a distant reminder of a violent past in this now most friendly and hospitable of houses.

Located in the village of Clonegal. NGR: S 913607. Open Sunday afternoons and by special appointment. (Write to Mrs Robertson, Huntington Castle, Clonegal, Co. Carlow.) Admission: free, although a small donation to the Fellowship of Isis would be appreciated.

MOUNT IEVERS COURT
County Clare

Like many of Ireland's tall eighteenth-century houses, Mount Ievers Court has a dream-like, melancholic quality that is positively beguiling. Set in lush parkland and sheltered by beech trees, the house rises three storeys over a basement, its height accentuated by a steeply pitched roof, tall chimney stacks and the subtle architectural devise of reducing the width of each storey by six inches. Each of its seven-bay fronts are almost identical, save one that is of silvery-grey limestone ashlar and the other of brick imported from Holland as ballast and now faded a beautiful shade of pink-grey. Its exquisite doll's house appearance is enhanced by string-coursing, quoins, lugged window surrounds and by small panes and heavy astragals in the window glazing – standard features of early eighteenth-century architecture.

Although Mount Ievers Court looks as if it was built around 1710, work did not in fact begin until 1731 when Colonel Henry Ievers demolished the seventeenth-century tower house that his grandfather Henry Ievers had acquired less than seventy years before. A stone fireplace dated 1648 was salvaged from the castle and re-erected in the hall of the house where it still stands. The architect of the new house was John

Rothery, whose son Isaac completed the work after his death in 1737. From a complete building account which survives, we know that eleven masons and forty-eight labourers were employed – the masons earning five shillings a week and the labourers only five pence, though each received food, drink, clothing and in some cases accommodation. Slates which cost nine shillings six pence per thousand came from Broadford ten miles away, while the massive oak-roof timbers, thirty-four tons in weight, came from Portumna, travelling by boat to Killaloe and hauled the twenty miles overland to Mount Ievers. With so much of the work relying on local labour and materials the cost of the house was only £1,478 7s. 9d. – a comparatively small amount by the standards of the time.

The interior of the house has a simple, restrained feel. Many rooms retain their contemporary panelling, including several in plaster that directly follow the lines of wood panelling. The ceilings, with their geometric panels and modillion cornices in the hall, the staircase and the upper hall are all reminiscent of Carolinian houses, as is the magnificent staircase with its fine joinery of alternate barley-sugar and fluted balusters. On the top floor is a long gallery possibly designed as a ball-room, a feature that is unique in Ireland – though Bowenscourt in County Cork once boasted one, a house also built by Isaac Rothery but tragically now demolished. The lovely chimney-pieces throughout the house, which include a Bossi, were installed around 1850 and are mostly late Georgian though the grates seem to be original to the house.

Other striking features include the fine brass knocker on the front door, the vaulted basements and a delightful 1740s fresco in the drawing-room giving a panoramic view of the house, demesne and landscape beyond. The formal garden landscape around the house has now largely disappeared, although the present owner of Mount Ievers, Squadron-Leader Norman Ievers, has restored the fish ponds represented in the fresco. He has also given the house a new roof and has done much to ensure that this magical building will survive into the next century.

Located just outside of Sixmilebridge, north east of Limerick. NGR: R 487663 Open by special appointment only. Tel: (061) 369126.

BANTRY HOUSE
County Cork

Bantry House is a theatrical place, full of drama and character. Standing at the foot of a steep terraced garden, it commands incomparable views across the waters of Bantry Bay to Whiddy Island and the Caha Mountains beyond. Its magnificent setting, like a Claude Lorraine painting, is matched by the many treasures of its interior – exquisite French furniture, tapestries and *objets d'art* – which give this remote Irish house the air of a continental baroque palace.

The original house, a five-bay three-storey building, was built by Samuel Hutchinson around 1720; called Blackrock, it forms the nucleus of the present Bantry House. In 1746 it was acquired by Richard White, a farmer from Whiddy Island who had amassed a fortune from pilchard-fishing, iron-smelting and probably from smuggling. Through a series of purchases, he acquired most of the land around Bantry including large parts of the Beare Peninsula – estates which were further enlarged by his grandson Richard White (1767–1851). The young Richard took little interest in social or political affairs, preferring to live quietly at Bantry, but in December 1796 he was unexpectedly thrust into the limelight when a French invasionary fleet sailed into Bantry Bay to join forces with the United Irishmen. White showed great initiative during the crisis by organising local defences and placing his home, then called Seafield, at the disposal of General Dalrymple who arrived with troops from Cork. Months after the would-be invasion, Richard White was created Baron Bantry in recognition of his 'spirited conduct and important service' during the crisis; in 1800 he was made a Viscount and in 1816 became the Earl of Bantry.

Although some modifications appear to have occurred during the 1770s, most of the additions and alterations took place during the first Earl's lifetime. A two-storey addition with bowed ends and a six-bay front facing onto Bantry Bay were added in 1820, providing space for two large drawing-rooms and several bedrooms above. Many more substantial changes were made in 1845 by Richard, Viscount Berehaven (1800–67) – a passionate art collector who travelled regularly across Europe, visiting Russia, Poland, France and Italy and bringing back shiploads of exotic goods between 1820 and 1840. To accommodate his new furnishings, the Viscount built a fourteen-bay block to the rear of the old house consisting of a six-bay centre of two storeys over a basement flanked by four-storey bow-ended wings. No doubt inspired by the grand baroque palaces of Germany, he gave the house a sense of architectural unity by lining the walls with giant red-brick pilasters with Coade-stone Corinthian capitals, the intervening spaces consisting of grey stucco and the parapet adorned with an attractive stone balustrade. He also laid out the Italianate gardens, including the magnificent terraces on the hillside behind the house, most of which was undertaken after he had succeeded his father as the second Earl of Bantry in 1851. After his death in 1867 the property was inherited by his brother William, the third Earl (1801–84), his grandson William, the fourth and last Earl (1854–91), and then passed through the female line to the present owner, Mr Shelswell-White.

Today, Bantry House remains much as the second Earl left it, with an important part of his great collection still intact. The rooms also retain their

The dining-room in Bantry House

Victorian clutter and no where more so than in the hall where visitors will find an array of bric-à-brac, including a mosque lamp from Damascus, an Arab chest, a Japanese inlaid chest, a Russian travelling shrine with fifteenth- and sixteenth-century icons, a Friesian clock and a sixteenth-century Spanish marriage chest. There is also a fine wooden seventeenth-century Flemish overmantel, rows of family portraits on the walls and the original standard of the 'Bantry Cavalry' which was raised in 1780 to defend the area against the French. The hall was created by combining two rooms with the staircase hall of the original house and consequently has a rather muddled shape, though crisp black-and-white Dutch floor tiles lend the room a sense of unity. Incorporated in this floor are four mosaic panels collected by Viscount Berehaven from Pompeii in 1828 and bearing the familiar inscriptions 'Cave Canem' and 'Salve'.

From the hall visitors enter the Rose and Gobelins drawing-rooms which offer magnificent vistas across the bay. Large windows and floor-to-ceiling mirrors have a marked regency appearance, though much of the furnishing actually comes from pre-Revolutionary France. The main features are the tapestries, which in the Rose drawing-room comprise four panels from the Royal Aubusson works, said to have been made for Marie Antoinette on her marriage to the Dauphin; the main subject is *fêtes champêtres* with insets apparently designed by the painter François Boucher and decorative surrounds by Tessier. The Gobelins tapestries in the adjacent room include one panel reputed to have been the property of Louis Philippe, Duc d'Orleans, cousin of Louis XV and grandfather of Louis Philippe of France at whose sale in 1851 this tapestry was bought. The deteriorating condition of these tapestries may sadden many visitors, as will the condition of other significant items in these rooms, such as the fragmenting Aubusson tapestry settee and chairs, the eighteenth-century Savonnerie carpet and the seventeenth-century Spanish leather wainscotting.

Undoubtedly the most spectacular room in the house is the dining-room, dominated by copies of Allan Ramsay's full-length portraits of George III and Queen Charlotte whose astonishingly elaborate gilt frames are well set off by the royal blue walls. The ceiling was once decorated with Guardi panels, but these have long since been removed and sold to passing dealers at a fraction of their worth. The differing heights of the room are due to the fact that they are partly incorporated in the original house and in the 1845 extension, their incongruity disguised by a screen of marble columns with gilded Corinthian capitals. Much of the furniture has been here since the time of the second Earl, including the fine George III dining table, Chippendale chairs, mahogany teapoy, immense sideboards made especially for the room and the enormous painting of 'The Fruit Market' by Snyders revealing figures reputedly drawn by Rubens – a wedding present to the first countess.

The first flight of the staircase from the hall belongs to the original early eighteenth-century house, as does the half-landing with its lugged architraves. This leads into the great library, built around 1845 and the last major addition to the house. The library is over sixty-feet long, has screens of marble Corinthian columns, a compartmented ceiling and Dublin-made marble mantelpieces at each end with overhanging mirrors. The furnishing is now rather spartan but retains a fine rosewood grand piano by Bluthner of Leipzig, still occasionally used for concerts. The windows of this room once looked into an immense glass conservatory, but this has now been removed and visitors will gaze out upon the recently restored gardens and the steep-sloping terraces behind. The imposing stable range with its pediment and cupola to one side of this garden has also been reconstructed and houses an exhibition entitled '1796 Armada Trust'.

Located on the outskirts of Bantry on the N71. NGR: V 988481. Open daily all year, except 25 December: 9.00 am – 6.00 pm. Open most spring and summer evenings until 8.00 pm. Tea room and craft shop open daily: 9.00 am – 5.30 pm. Toilet facilities. Admission: adults IR £2.50; senior citizens and students IR £1.50; children under 14 free with parents; adult groups of 20+ IR £2.00. Bed-and-breakfast accommodation also available: IR £45.00 – £55.00 p.p. Tel: (027) 50047.

DUNKATHEL

County Cork

During the late eighteenth century, successful Cork merchants built a string of elegant villas along the banks of the Lee Estuary. Many of these have now disappeared, but one which still survives intact is Dunkathel, alias Dunkettle, a solid neo-classical house with an idyllic parkland setting lying just below the mouth of the Glanmire River.

Dunkathel was built around 1785 for Abraham Morris in the Palladian manner, with a two-storey nine-bay centre block linked to office wings by screen walls with rusticated niches. Although stylistically in the manner of the Sardinian architect Davis Duckart, the building was almost certainly designed by his pupil Abraham Hargrove of Cork. It replaced the early eighteenth-century mansion of the Trant family, part of which still survives, notably some plasterwork in one of the courtyard ranges behind the house.

·   The fanlighted front door, flanked by engaged Tuscan columns, leads directly into the entrance hall which occupies the whole centre of the building. As at Florence Court, this room is divided into two parts by a segmented archway, thus allowing the magnificent bifurcated staircase of Bath stone with its attractive iron balustrades to be admired immediately upon entering the house. A huge round-headed window over the half-landing lights both the hall and the bedroom landing above. The outer portion of the hall retains its early nineteenth-century marbled Siena-like walls and its ceilings with painted blue sky and clouds. On the left is a fine marble chimney-piece and opposite, a magnificent gilt mirror – one of a number in this house. Close by is a grand piano and against the wall in the staircase hall stands a rare barrel organ, designed by Imhoff and Muckle in 1880 and still played for visitors with much musical vigour.

The main reception rooms flanking the hall are entered through polished wooden doors with lugged architraves – a rather late feature for a house of this date. To the right is the dining-room whose green-painted walls are lined with the ancestral portraits of the Russell family, now the owners of the house, and their relatives the Wise-Gubbins who purchased Dun-kathel from Jonas Morris around 1870. For many years the house was the home of the five Gubbins sisters, all of whom were deaf, until the Russell family inherited when the Gubbins line ran out of heirs. In the drawing-room on the opposite side of the hall are some of the unique Victorian watercolours by Beatrice Gubbins, an indefatigable traveller. Like other rooms in the house it has a bright, spacious feel, though perhaps rather oddly is currently used by the family as a fabric shop.

Located 3½ miles from Cork on the Waterford–Rosslare Road (N25). NGR: W 732730. Open May to mid October: Wednesdays to Sundays, 2.00 – 6.00 pm; or by appointment. Antiques and gifts for sale. Afternoon teas available. Toilet facilities. Admission: adults IR £2.00; senior citizens and students IR £1.50; children IR £1.00. Special group rates available. Tel: (021) 821014.

FOTA HOUSE

County Cork

The demesne of Fota, or Foaty Island, contributes enormously to the beauty of the Lee Estuary whose sublimity moved Lady Chatterton to write in 1838: 'the sun always seems to shine brighter here than else-where'. Fota's magnificent parkland, its gardens and splendid mansion – one of Ireland's finest regency houses – combine to create an aura of charm and serenity apparent to all who visit.

Fota's former owners, the Smith-Barrys, were direct descendants of Philip de Barry, a Norman settler who was granted lands in Cork in 1179. The main branch of this family, the Earls of Barrymore, lived at Barryscourt about one mile east of Fota until 1630 when they moved to Castle Lyons, some fifteen miles to the north. Their great estates were later ruined by the reckless gambling of 'Hellgate', the seventh Earl of Barrymore, but Fota was unaffected by this debacle for it had earlier been given to Arthur, third son of the fourth Earl. In the 1750s Arthur built a five-bay hunting box on Fota and after his death in 1770 the property passed to his wealthy younger brother John, and later in turn to his eldest son James Hugh Smith-Barry of Marbury, Cheshire. James spent much of his time hunting and racing in England, only using Fota occasionally, but his eldest son John, who inherited the property in 1801, had a rather different attitude to his Irish home. John had a passion for sailing and from an early age preferred to live at Fota where he could race with the Royal Cork Yacht Club. As soon as he came of age in 1814 he married an Irish girl from Ballyedmund and decided to make Fota Island his principal seat.

Initially, John Smith-Barry planned to build a new residence on a more elevated site on Fota and commis-sioned the Irish architect Richard Morrison and his son William Vitruvius to design a mansion in the new Tudor Revival style. This was later rejected and in the early 1820s the Morrisons were engaged to alter and extend the old Georgian box. They added two pedi-mented wings to either side of the old house, built a Doric portico and remodelled the interior in the rich classical regency style it retains to this day. They also constructed a long two-storey service range to one side of the house and helped to create the park, demesne wall, gatelodges and other demesne buildings. John Smith-Barry, however, did not have long to enjoy his splendid new seat and died in 1837, barely eight years after it was finished. He had lived lavishly, earning him the nickname 'John the Magnificent', but his son James Hugh reacted against this and rarely visited Fota until after his marriage in 1841. Later, James spent more time at Fota where he established the famous arboretum, and just before his early death in 1856 he completed the billiard-room wing at the end of the service range – built in the same style as the Morrison wings but with only one storey. The area between the billiard room and the main building was filled in, during 1890, with a single-storey range containing a long gallery – the inspiration of Arthur Smith-Barry, first and last Lord Barrymore (1843–1925).

Fota was later inherited by Lord Barrymore's son-in-law and daughter, Major and the Honourable Mrs Bell, who sold Marbury, the family seat in Cheshire, and moved their valuable picture collection to Fota. Upon Mrs Bell's death in 1975, however, the pictures were returned to England and Fota was acquired by University College, Cork, principally for use as a dairy research centre. The house was saved from an uncertain fate in 1976 when it was leased by local businessman Richard Woods, who was looking for somewhere to display his collection of eighteenth- and nineteenth-century Irish pictures, mostly landscapes, that he had been acquiring since 1970. In 1983 the house was exquisitely redecorated by John O'Connell with Irish furniture and fittings to complement the Woods collection and was opened to the public.

Visitors are often surprised by the wealth of sumptuous decorative detail in the house, for the simplicity of the building's exterior gives no hint of what lies within. The entrance hall takes up the entire front of the old house and is divided by screens of yellow scagliola columns whose Ionic capitals support lintels decorated with wreaths alternating with the Barry crest. Together with the ceiling they are painted a white-grey, matching the faded green colour of the walls and the columns – cast for a group of busts collected by Woods.

The hall extends into anterooms at each end, giving access to the main reception rooms of the house. In the north wing lies the dining-room while to the south are the library and the big drawing-room. The dining-room is a classic Morrison masterpiece with rich and crisply moulded frieze ornamentation and dark green scagliola columns, while the magnificent new curtains were inspired from Irish drawings of 1843. Even more impressive are the richly draped valances in the library, but these are originals dating to around 1830 that were rescued from Ballynagall – a splendid house near Mullingar that has since fallen into ruin. The library walls are lined with pictures of the Irish school, including three by William Ashford (1746–1824), notably his famed composition of Cloughoughter Castle. The mouldings of the frieze and ceiling surround, like those of the dining-room, have been left uncoloured and ungilded, but similar ornamented plasterwork in the adjacent drawing-room, which extends into one of the bows of the front garden, was redecorated in the 1870s following a partial ceiling collapse. This was carried out by Sibthorpe of Dublin and includes stencilled decoration and panels of paper which give the whole room an opulent appearance typical of the late Victorian era. The blue walls were copied from the ground colour of the ceiling, while the paintings include landscapes by Robert Carver, Thomas Roberts and George Mullins.

Some of the best plasterwork in the house can be found in the staircase hall opposite the main entrance. The stairs, with their brass banisters, rise beneath an enriched shallow dome, while a pair of columns on the top landing flank an attractive vista to a secondary flight that leads to the top storey. Several of the bedrooms contain further pictures and one still preserves its mid nineteenth-century wallpaper. Many of the best pictures in the house, however, are to be found in the watercolour room off the hall and visitors should inspect this room before leaving the house. It contains eighteenth- and nineteenth-century drawings and watercolours grouped around the walls and includes the charming well-known watercolour of 'The Dry Bridge at Blarney' by the Cork artist Nathanial Grogan.

The redecoration of Fota and its adaptation as the home for the Woods picture collection is undoubtedly one of the success stories of Irish conservation. Unfortunately, Fota has recently been sold to an English development company who has received planning permission to construct hotels, golf courses and numerous holiday dwellings on this lovely island. Although the house, arboretum and seventy acres of parkland were withdrawn from the developers' plans (after public protest), the future of the house remains very much in doubt. It is now managed by the Fota Trust who closed the building to the public at the end of 1990, due to the deterioration of its structure.

Located on Fota Island 9 miles east of Cork city on the Cobh Road. NGR: W 790715. Since this entry was written, the fabric of the house has deteriorated in the absence of any maintenance programme. The house is now closed to the public and the long-term future of the Woods collection is under discussion. The wildlife park and arboretum remain open to visitors. Car park for all amenities IR £1.50 per car. Tour coaches free. Tel: (021) 812728.

CASTLE WARD
County Down

One of the most interesting aspects of country house design lies in the decorative schemes adopted for the male and female spheres of the building; the drawing-room and boudoir are often feminine and adventurous in taste, while the hall and dining-room are predominantly conservative. Such divisions were generally confined to plasterwork and furnishings, but at Castle Ward they have been incorporated into the architecture itself, with the adoption of the fashionable Strawberry Hill Gothick for the female rooms in contrast to the conventional classicism of the male preserves. The choice of Gothick inevitably meant the creation of a suitable façade to accommodate the pointed windows; the garden front overlooking Strangford Lough is in the Gothick taste with ogee- and centre-pointed windows and a battlemented parapet with pinnacles, whereas the entrance elevation is textbook Palladian with a rusticated ground floor and a three-bay pediment featuring engaged columns – a contrast which makes Castle Ward one of the most memorable eighteenth-century houses in Ireland.

Sadly, little documentary evidence has survived relating to the building of the house, though it is clear that work began in 1761 and lasted until 1767. It was commissioned by Bernard Ward, later first Viscount Bangor (1719–81), whose family first settled in the area around 1570 when they built the original Castle Ward – a tower house which stands in the farmyard close to the shore. This castle was replaced in 1710 by a new mansion constructed a short distance north west by

Arms of the third Viscount over music-room door,
Castle Ward

Bernard's father, Judge Michael Ward (1683–1759) – a
remarkable figure who achieved great wealth through
marriage and business acumen. His house no longer
stands, but much of its surrounding formal landscape
survives, notably the impressive Temple Water dug in
the 1720s. Bernard proved to be no less energetic than
his father and began creating a 'naturalistic' landscape
park as a setting for his new house before his father's
death in 1759 – no doubt encouraged by his wife Lady
Anne Bligh, daughter of the first Earl of Darnley. Work
on the house was well underway when Mrs Delany
visited in July 1762 and expressed concern that its

25

magnificent setting 'should not be judiciously laid out. He wants taste and Lady Anne is so whimsical that I doubt her judgement. If they do not do too much they can't spoil the place for it hath every advantage from nature that can be desired.'

Mrs Delany need not have worried for the park was laid out in excellent taste, while the house is an attractive and highly accomplished piece of architecture. The architect's identity remains a mystery – it is generally accepted that he was not Irish but could have been any one of several dozen competent architects operating in England at that time. His plan was a rectangle with semi-octagonal bays at each end, the façades being built of Bath stone which Bernard had used when erecting Lady Anne's Temple around 1750. Contrary to popular mythology, Bernard and his wife worked closely together on the design of the house; indeed, there is every reason to suppose that Bernard thoroughly approved of the Gothick style, particularly as it gave substance to the name Castle Ward. Furthermore, Lady Anne never left her husband as is often claimed but remained with him at Castle Ward until his death in 1781.

Main staircase at Castle Ward

After Bernard's death the estate was placed in Chancery due to the insanity of Nicholas, the second Viscount. Nicholas continued to live at Castle Ward while the third son, Robert, received Bangor Castle and a substantial estate. Edward, the second son, moved into Castle Ward as guardian to his brother and was given an allowance for the upkeep of the house and demesne. This arrangement might have worked had Robert not been one of the three people appointed to manage the revenue of the estate. Robert was jealous of Edward and refused to increase the allowance after it proved insufficient. Edward, who had little money of his own, sank increasingly into poverty and resorted to farming the park to make money. At one stage he even tried selling bread at the gate, and eventually died a broken man in 1812. His elder brother Nicholas lived on until 1827 by which time Robert had removed most of Castle Ward's contents to Bangor, leaving only the ancestral portraits, while the demesne remained in a state of ruin. Much of the present decoration and furnishing consequently dates from the 1830s when Edward's son – Edward Southwell, the third Viscount (1790–1857) – refurbished the interior. The only subsequent work of note was carried out by the fourth Viscount (1827–81) when the main entrance was moved to the eastern bay in 1870 and a porch was added.

The old hall, later converted to a music room, is richly decorated with a screen of scagliola Doric columns, a fine marble fireplace and a late nineteenth-century parquet floor, which replaced the original seen by Sir James Caldwell on his visit in 1722 and referred to as 'inlaid with oak and mahogany and diced and kept smooth with rubbing and beeswax that you are in danger of slipping every moment'. The most remarkable feature of the room is the plasterwork, especially the very decorative festoons of musical instruments and gardening tools which were added to the earlier more formal work in 1828 by a local plasterer, Graham of Dundrum, who cut corners by incorporating real objects into the design.

The two rooms flanking the old hall are also in the classical style. Of these the library is not an especially distinguished room, though it does contain one of William Ashford's finest landscapes – a view from the temple across the park at Castle Ward, dated 1785. The dining-room, which Sir James Caldwell rightly observed was 'quite too small for such a house', is an attractive room with painted, grained and gilded panelling and has a chimney-piece with a charming relief panel of Ceres and Cupid frolicking amongst vine leaves. Above the fireplace is an unusual portrait group painted at the Bishop's Palace at Dromore, probably by Thomas Robinson, while also in the room is a portrait of poor Edward Ward attributed to Romney.

The main Gothick room in the house is the saloon in the centre of the east front – most striking for the rich quality of its decoration, with a ceiling of fretting and quatrefoils, pointed doors and an overmantel with battlemented top. The adjacent sitting-room or boudoir is the most astonishing room of the house because of its spectacular ceiling with huge udder-like pendentives, which according to a contemporary letter are based on Henry VII's chapel at Westminster Abbey. This room lies adjacent to the main staircase, notable for its elegant wrought-iron balustrade with S-scrolls of the type popularised by Sir William Chambers. It occupies a bay in the middle of the north-west façade and gives access to the bedroom floor, the mid Victorian entrance porch and the basement.

On their way out through the basement, visitors will find a special room dedicated to the memory of Mary Ward (1827–69), one of the most fascinating people associated with Castle Ward. Born Mary King, the daughter of a rector in Offaly, she was a botanical artist and outstanding naturalist who published a number of books connected with the microscope. She married Henry Ward (1828–1911) in 1854 but died before he succeeded his brother as fifth Viscount in 1881. With the death of her eldest son Maxwell Ward, sixth Viscount Bangor (1868–1950), Castle Ward was given in lieu of death duties to the National Trust who have continued to maintain the house in excellent condition.

Located 1 mile west of Strangford on the Downpatrick Road (A25). NGR: J 573494. House open April, September and October: weekends, 1.00 – 6.00 pm. Open daily during Easter: 1.00 – 6.00 pm. Open daily from May to August, except Thursdays: 1.00 – 6.00 pm. Estate and grounds open daily from dawn to dusk. Restaurant and gift shop in stableyard open as house. Toilet facilities. Admission to house: adults £2.50; children £1 .25; groups £2.00. Admission to estate: £3.00 per car (November to end March, £1.50 per car). Tel: (039686) 204.

MOUNT STEWART

County Down

Social entertainment was always an important part of country house life and nowhere more so than at Mount Stewart, whose luxuriously appointed and sun-filled apartments were once the setting for a succession of glittering house parties that sometimes even included royalty. The Marquesses of Londonderry were fabulously rich and although they had an English seat and a palatial house in Park Lane, regularly came back to Mount Stewart where they continued their role as prominent political hosts. Their house, a long, low and deceptively large classical building overlooking Strangford Lough, has undergone many changes by successive generations of the family, most recently by Edith, wife of the seventh Marquess, during the interwar years. It retains its comfortable house-party atmosphere, while its famous formal gardens created by Edith as an extension to the reception rooms remain much as she left them.

The Stewarts achieved their enormous wealth largely through astute marriage arrangements. Originally, the family settled near Moville where they had been granted lands in the seventeenth century, but in 1737 Alexander Stewart (1700–81) married Mary Cowan, an heiress with shares in the East India Company. With her fortune he purchased the demesne lands of Mount Stewart in 1744, originally known as Mount Pleasant, and built a house there. His son Robert (1739–1821) consolidated the family's fortune and social influence and was created first Marquess of Londonderry in 1816. He employed James 'Athenian' Stuart to build the Temple of the Winds above Strangford Lough between 1782 and 1785; later,

The central hall at Mount Stewart

between 1804 and 1806, he engaged the London architect George Dance to design what is now the west wing of the mansion. Nearly two decades earlier Wyatt had been brought in to remodel his father's house, but Wyatt's designs were never to be realised as so much money was spent getting the young Robert Stewart elected as MP for County Down – an election which turned out to be a good investment since Stewart, later Lord Castlereagh and second Marquess of Londonderry (1769–1822), rose to be Foreign Secretary, leader of the House of Commons at Westminster and perhaps the greatest political figure of his generation.

Lord Castlereagh committed suicide in 1822 and the family estates were inherited by his half-brother Charles, the third Marquess (1778–1854). A few years earlier he had married Lady Frances Anne Vane-Tempest, heiress to one of England's richest families with vast estates and collieries in the north of England. Although the new Marquess now found his time divided between a string of country seats in England and the palatial Holderness – later Londonderry House in Park Lane – he nevertheless engaged the celebrated Irish architect William Vitruvius Morrison to rebuild and enlarge Mount Stewart in 1835. The work was finished around 1840, some two years after Morrison's death, and comprised a large new block to the rear of the old house with an eleven-bay entrance front and pedimented *porte cochère*. The new work was designed so that it matched Dance's earlier building and a balustraded roof parapet was added to give the whole house a sense of unity.

The main door of the entrance hall leads into the principal interior feature of Morrison's house – a great central hall with an octagonal balustraded gallery lit from above through a dome filled with stained glass. The room now features pieces of sculpture, as it was probably originally intended to, while display cabinets contain a striking Chinese Export armorial service with the arms of Sir Robert Cowan, Governor of Bombay, whose fortune provided the Stewarts with the means to acquire the house in 1744. In mid Victorian times, however, the fourth Marquess (1805–72) had this chamber filled with over 3,000 antlers, a wide variety of animal heads, heraldic banners and suits of armour. By all accounts the fourth Marquess, who undertook an adventurous expedition to the Middle East in 1842, was quite a romantic; it was he who built Scrabo Tower overlooking Newtownards during the 1850s in memory of his father.

A passage from the central hall leads to the core of Dance's earlier house – an imperial staircase with stone treads, wrought-iron balusters and a ramped mahogany handrail. The roof is lit by an octagonal skylight dome with segmental arch supports that is typical of Dance and of his famous pupil Sir John Soane. Below are large display cases filled with a variety of fine porcelain, part of a large collection at Mount Stewart. The dominant feature of the room, however, and perhaps the most important picture in Ireland is the magnificent 'Hambletonian', the masterpiece by George Stubbs that was moved here from Londonderry House during the last war. It depicts a racehorse owned by Sir Henry Vane-Tempest being rubbed down after it had just beaten Joseph Cookson's horse Diamond at Newmarket in 1799.

Music-room door, Mount Stewart

Adjacent to the staircase hall is the music room, which lies at the centre of the west front, flanked by the sitting-room and the Castlereagh room. All three rooms remain very much as Dance had left them, particularly the music room with its delicate ceiling of pendentives and its oak and mahogany floor with central inlaid patera – almost certainly the work of John Ferguson who was responsible for the outstanding marquetry on the floor of the upper room in the Temple of the Winds. The flanking Castlereagh room, originally the dining-room and later the library, has been filled by the

National Trust with items relevant to the life and times of Lord Castlereagh – the 'Winston Churchill' of British politics during and after the Napoleonic War.

Morrison's principal reception rooms – the dining-room and the drawing-room – flank the south and north elevations respectively. They are both spacious, long, rectangular rooms, but the dining-room has subsequently been shortened by the incorporation of a kitchen at the east end, beyond a screen of Ionic columns. The room is still impressive, however, and ranged against the walls are the twenty-two Empire chairs which were used by the delegates to the Congress of Vienna in 1815; the backs and seats of the chairs were embroidered by nuns in Nantes for Edith, seventh Marchioness, depicting the arms of those present and the nations they represented. Above the chairs hang life-sized portraits by Sir Godfrey Kneller of the first Earl and Countess of Albermarle, forebears of Lady Mairi Bury's late husband and Edith's son-in-law. King Edward and Queen Alexander would have dined here when they visited Mount Stewart in 1903. One wonders whether the sixth Marquess, in the presence of the King, indulged his famed habit of eating dinner as rapidly as possible – a habit which understandably made him very unpopular with guests whose plates were often whisked away by footmen before they had tasted anything.

The vast drawing-room, with Ionic column screens at each end, remains much as it was after being decorated in the 1930s by Edith, seventh Marchioness, who like her mother-in-law before her was one of the great political hostesses of the time. The furnishing comprises quite a mixture of pieces from different periods, including Carrara marble urns and vases, tripod candlesticks carved with winged lions, standard lamps, sofas, armchairs, occasional tables – all grouped informally as if the house guests were expected to return at any moment. It is perhaps sad that they never will, but the house and its remarkable gardens are now wonderfully maintained by the National Trust for all to enjoy.

Located 5 miles south east of Newtownards on the Portaferry Road (A20). NGR: J 552698. House open April and October: weekends only, 1.00 – 6.00 pm. Open daily during Easter: 1.00 – 6.00 pm. Open daily from May to September, except Tuesdays: 1.00 – 6.00 pm. Gardens open daily, April to September: 10.30 am – 6.00 pm; open weekends only during October, 10.30 am – 6.00 pm. Gift shop and tea room open April, May, September and October: weekends, 1.30 – 5.30 pm. Open daily during Easter: 1.30 – 5.30 pm. Open bank holidays: 1.00 – 6.00 pm. Open daily from June to August, except Tuesdays: 1.30 – 5.30 pm; Sundays, 1.30 – 6.00 pm. Toilet facilities. Admission to house, gardens and temple: adults £3.30; children £1.65; groups £2.60. Admission to gardens and temple: adults £2.70; children £1.35; groups £2.00. Admission to temple only: £0.90. Tel: (024774) 387.

MALAHIDE CASTLE
County Dublin

Such was the troubled state of Ireland's past that few Irish country houses were ever continuously inhabited by the same family for more than a few centuries. A rare exception to this rule was Malahide Castle – home of the Talbots for 791 years. Granted in 1185 to Richard Talbot, one of the knights who arrived in Ireland with Henry II in 1174, the property remained in Talbot hands until 1976 when it was acquired by Dublin County Council. Unfortunately, the Irish government was unwilling to accept the property in lieu of death duties, and its remarkable collection of portraits and furniture, which uniquely reflected Ireland's historical and cultural development, had to be sold by auction. Fortunately, Ireland's tourist board, Bord Failte, managed to purchase much of the furniture at the sale together with the castle's carpets and curtains, and these remain at Malahide alongside thirty-five portraits bought by the National Gallery of Ireland. Further important acquisitions of Irish furniture have been added to the collection so that Malahide's interior still retains much of its old beauty and magic.

The core of the medieval castle is the oak room, approached by a winding stone staircase and lit by Gothic windows added in 1820 when the room was enlarged and the front hall below was created. The room contains fine carved panelling, mostly of sixteenth-century date, which has darkened to a gleaming ebony. Some of the carving is of Flemish origin, including six exquisite panels representing biblical scenes opposite the window; their religious theme suggests that the Talbots, who remained Roman Catholics until 1774, used this room as a chapel in penal times. According to tradition, the Flemish carving of the coronation of the virgin over the mantelpiece disappeared when the castle was occupied by the Cromwellian Miles Corbet between 1653 and 1660. Fortunately for the Talbots, the unsavory Corbet was one of the regicides who signed the death warrant of Charles I and after the Restoration he was duly hung, drawn and quartered at Tyburn. Samuel Pepys recorded the occasion in his diary on 19 April 1662: 'This morning before we sat, I went to Aldgate and at the corner shop, a draper's, I stood and did see Barkestead, Okey and Corbet drawn towards the gallows.' The Talbots returned to Malahide and the figure of the virgin made a miraculous reappearance above the fireplace. Until 1976 the room contained James Boswell's ebony cabinet in which were found over 1,000 manuscript pages of Boswell's *Life of Johnson* in the 1920s.

The thick walls of the oak room are flanked on the east side by the great hall, added to the castle around 1475. Unique in Ireland, this great hall not only retained its original form but also remained in domestic use as a dining-room until 1976. Its vaulted undercroft and corbel heads of Edward IV are original, but during the nineteenth century it was given a new roof, mantels and a minstrels' gallery. The furniture and pictures are of mostly seventeenth- and eighteenth-century date. The magnificent thirty-five-foot table comes from Powerscourt but many other items are original, including the nucleus of the Talbot ancestral portraits acquired by the National Gallery – a collection that is unusual since most of the Talbots' ancestors were Jacobites rather than the supporters of King William who usually decorate Irish country houses. Some valuable pictures were lost to this room in 1976, but the National Gallery managed to acquire a very fine John Michael Wright of Lady Catherine and Lady Charlotte Talbot. To replace lost pictures along the side wall, the National Gallery loaned the huge 'Battle of the Boyne' by Wyck – a superb picture that not only suits this room visually but is historically appropriate; on the morning of the Battle of the Boyne fourteen

Talbot cousins, all followers of James II, gathered here to dine – none survived the carnage of the day.

The west side of the castle is occupied by an early seventeenth-century addition which once contained four tapestry-hung chambers. The wing was burnt around 1760 and these rooms were subsequently replaced with two fine drawing-rooms, while externally the architect added round corner turrets, giving the house a Georgian Gothick character. The two rooms were given splendid rococo plasterwork ceilings; the life-like mouldings in the coves of the smaller drawing-room are attributable on stylistic grounds to the great Dublin stuccodore Robert West. Above all, however, these drawing-rooms are famous for their wonderful nineteenth-century painted orange-terracotta walls that many have apparently attempted to reproduce without success over the years. The colour makes an ideal background for the gilt frames of the fine pictures that grace the walls. Of particular note is the splendid portrait of Nathaniel Hone and Sir Joshua Reynold's portrait of Edmund Burke. The larger drawing-room retains its lovely Chinese carpet and also boasts two French-style gilt settees circa 1770 and a pair of George II Irish giltwood sideboards with black lacquered tops. The sideboards had been acquired at the auction by an international art dealer who was just about to pass them on to an Iranian client when he was persuaded to sell them back to Malahide. The delightful little turret rooms with ogee Gothic windows beside the two drawing-rooms have long been used to feature small pictures and miniatures. In one hangs a set of Trench family portraits – six pastels and twelve oils by Hugh Douglas Hamilton in frames possibly designed by Gandon.

The great hall at Malahide Castle

The famous gardens around the castle are largely the creation of the late Lord Talbot de Malahide who died suddenly in April 1973. They have been well restored by Dublin County Council and are certainly worth visiting. Also in the castle yard is the Cyril Fry Model Railway Exhibition with its model engines, rolling stock and replicas of railway stations in Dublin, Belfast and Cork.

Located in Malahide, 9 miles north of Dublin. NGR: O 220452. Open daily, April to October: weekdays, 10.00 am – 5.00 pm; Saturdays, 11.00 am – 6.00 pm; Sundays 2.00 – 6.00 pm. November to May: Saturdays, Sundays and bank holidays, 2.00 – 5.00 pm. Toilet facilities. Admission to castle: adults IR £2.45; senior citizens and students IR £1.85; children IR £1.25; groups IR £2.10. Admission to model railway: adults IR £2.00; senior citizens and students IR £1.45; children IR £1.15. Tel: castle (01) 452655; model railway (01) 452758.

NEWBRIDGE HOUSE
County Dublin

Although located within a few miles of Dublin's advancing urban sprawl, Newbridge House still manages to preserve its character of a secluded eighteenth-century gentleman's residence set in a wooded demesne. The house features a series of beautifully proportioned rooms, each retaining their original furnishings thanks to an agreement between the Cobbe family and its new owners, Dublin City Council, who acquired the property in 1986 and have since embarked on a major restoration of the house, yards and parkland.

The front façade of Newbridge is particularly attractive. A facing of pink ashlar gives it a lovely warm glow, while the use of a high basement, solid roof parapet, shouldered window architraves and tripartite doorway within a two-storey six-bay composition is also undoubtedly a success. For many years Newbridge was believed to be the work of Richard Castle, but we now know that it was designed by the prominent Dublin architect George Semple and built between 1749 and 1750 for Archbishop Charles Cobbe on land acquired in 1736.

Charles Cobbe (1686–1765) first came to Ireland in

1717 as chaplain to his cousin – the Lord Lieutenant and second Duke of Bolton. Despite a limited intellectual capacity he enjoyed rapid promotion through three minor bishoprics and became Archbishop of Dublin in 1742. His portrait hangs in the hall and shows him wearing a long grey wig and a black sleeveless surplice over the full lawn sleeves of a bishop. He died in 1765 and the house was inherited by his son Thomas and his fashionable wife, Lady Betty Beresford, sister of the first Marquis of Waterford. They built a wing at the back of the house to accommodate a huge drawing-room for entertaining and a gallery to house their growing collection of pictures and statuary. The drawing-room was subsequently redecorated by Thomas's grandson in the regency style and the house has since remained remarkably unaltered.

The front façade of Newbridge House

Conventionally, the hall has a masculine and conservative appearance with a strong architectural character that would be entirely at home in any house two decades earlier. Prominent features include a bold modillion cornice, wall panelling, bold dado rails and skirting boards, lugged architraves, and a large pedimented chimney-piece incorporating the Cobbe coat of arms. Here in this room guests would have been received and business transacted with tradesmen. To the right lies the dining-room dominated by its original black Kilkenny marble chimney-piece, a survival of a post 1765 redecoration of the room which saw a rococo ceiling, plaster wall panels and festoons installed. The Greek key pattern of these panels is reflected in the two Irish Chippendale sideboards which were made especially for the room. The chairs surrounding the large dining-room table all have the Cobbe family crest; above is a magnificent chandelier whose glittering crystal would have been reflected in the elaborate mirror on the wall.

Other rooms in the main building include the library, with its baroque ceiling depicting the four seasons, and the 'Mr Cobbe's Museum or Cabinet of Curiosities' – a curio room dating from 1790 and containing a remarkable display of souvenirs and trophies collected by various members of the family on their numerous travels abroad, particularly in India. The cabinets are original, as is the attractive and recently restored wallcover above, made of bamboo and Chinese paper.

From the museum visitors proceed into the middle hall which forms the north-west corner of the old house. An arch in the end wall guides the eye through a narrow vestibule to the richly modelled pedimented doorcase framing the door of the red drawing-room, which was added by the archbishop's son after 1765. This is a vast room, 42.9 feet by 25.6 feet with a bowed window looking out onto the gardens and an elaborate rococo ceiling and coved cornice by Richard William, a pupil of the great stuccodore Robert West. The room was redecorated in 1828 and still retains its carpet, crimson flock wallpaper and curtains, the latter made by the Dublin firm Mack, Williams and Gibton who also supplied much of the room's furniture. The walls have no less than forty-five pictures, many bought on the advice of the art connoisseur Matthew Pilkington, Vicar of Donabate. Pilkington was a friend of Cobbe's and is best remembered for his spectacular divorce suit with his wife, the amusing and naughty Laetitia, who was described by Virginia Woolf in an essay as 'shady, shifting and adventurous'. Mrs Pilkington's autobiography is on display in one of the glass cases in the house.

The servants' rooms in the basement and yard have also survived intact and have been admirably restored in recent years. The kitchen is fitted with its original screen wall, dresser with jugs and dishes, mid nineteenth-century iron range, whiskey still, duck press, rat traps, numerous copper pots, jelly moulds and wooden tub for salting meat. In the adjacent laundry visitors can inspect a range of equipment used to wash,

The kitchen at Newbridge House

dry, iron and mend clothes. In the cobbled yard lies the dairy with its marble niches for maturing cheeses, the demesne workers' kitchen, a forge and a carpenter's shop. On display in the coach house is the state carriage made in London in 1790 for 'Black Jack' FitzGibbon, the Lord Chancellor of Ireland and a relation of the Cobbes. The coach was itself black until restored by the National Museum to its former gold magnificence – even the fresco panels had been painted out, probably for the funeral of Queen Victoria.

Located on the western edge of Donabate, 11 miles north of Dublin on the N1. NGR: O 214501. Open April to October: Tuesdays to Fridays, 10.00 am – 5.00 pm; Saturdays, 11.00 am – 6.00 pm; Sundays and bank holidays, 2.00 – 6.00 pm. November to March: weekends and bank holidays, 2.00–5.00 pm. Coffee shop. Toilet facilities. Admission: adults IR £2.35, groups IR £2.10; senior citizens and students IR £2.00, groups IR £1.80; children IR £1.25, groups IR £1.15; family ticket IR £6.75. Tel: (01) 8436534/5.

CASTLE COOLE

County Fermanagh

By the end of the eighteenth century the classicism of
Palladio with its Renaissance interpretations of Roman
buildings had been replaced by the neo-classical movement proclaiming the primitive virtues, simplicity and
tranquil grandeur of Greek architecture. Although
Castle Coole still has echoes of Palladianism in its
balustraded roof parapets, Venetian windows and
centre block with wings, it is without doubt the most
perfect neo-classical country house in the British Isles –
the masterpiece of James Wyatt whose brilliant adoption of earlier designs by Richard Johnson resulted in a
monumental, masculine and chaste house enhanced by
a gleaming white façade of Portland stone. Its magnificence so impressed the French traveller de Latocraye,
when shown around the house in 1797 by its proud
new owner, the first Earl of Belmore, that he considered
this 'superb palace' to be too splendid for ordinary
morals, remarking that it was better 'to leave temples to
the gods'.

The demesne lands of Castle Coole originally
belonged to the Maguires, whose crannog on the lake
was abandoned in 1611 when the lands were granted to
Roger Atkinson, an English adventurer who built a
castle close to the lake shore. The property changed
hands a number of times until purchased in 1656 by
John Corry, a Belfast merchant of Scottish origin. His
son James Corry (1643–1718) replaced the castle in
1709 with a fine Queen Anne house, whose garden
layout is still visible 400 yards north west of the present
house together with its canal and splendid oak avenue,
planted in 1725. After Armar Lowry-Corry (1740–
1802) inherited the property through his mother in
1774 he determined to build a much grander house to
match his considerable wealth, accumulated through
three marriages, and his rising status as Baron (1781),
Viscount (1789) and Earl of Belmore (1797).

Work levelling the site for the new house began in
the autumn of 1788; in October 1789 the Dublin
architect Richard Johnson submitted plans, and work
on the basement commenced. Seven months later, for
some unknown reason, Lord Belmore transferred
patronage to James Wyatt who adopted Johnson's
plan, improved his elevation in 1790 and worked on
the house until it was completed in November 1798.
Wyatt operated from London and through Alexander
Stewart, the clerk of works, he controlled every aspect

Castle Coole dining-room

of the operation, including the internal fittings, the plasterwork and even the design of the furniture. No expense was spared in getting the finest materials and craftsmen available – Portland stone was specially shipped from Dorset for the exterior cladding, and the gangs of imported artificers on site must have seemed like a veritable factory – fourteen joiners, twenty-five stone cutters, twenty-six masons, ten stone sawyers, seventeen carpenters and eighty-three labourers. When completed the cost amounted to £54,000, nearly twice the original estimate, with the result that the first Earl found himself in debt and unable to furnish all of the principal rooms. This task was thus undertaken by his son Somerset, the second Earl (1774–1841), who brought up the leading Dublin upholsterer of the time, John Preston of Henry Street; at a cost of over £17,000, Preston furnished and decorated the rooms in a bold and opulent 'Grecian manner' between 1807 and 1825. In 1817 the second Earl also engaged Sir Richard Morrison to build the impressive stableyard – another project his father had been unable to undertake, though the vaulted tunnel linking the yard to the basement had been completed in 1790.

The sense of proportion, spaciousness and high-quality craftsmanship that visitors will experience in the entrance hall is repeated throughout the house. The room remains much as Wyatt intended except for the recently restored porphyry-red of the walls, which copies a scrape of the colour specified by Preston around 1816. This colour blends well with the screen of red scagliola columns (by the Italian Dominic Bartoli), which support a full Doric entablature running round the room. The bare walls, Portland stone flagging, statues in the wall niches and curtainless windows combine to give the hall a cool, austere, neo-classical feel in striking contrast to the great oval saloon in the middle of the garden front – by far the richest room in the house and one of the most magnificent in Ireland. The ceiling of this room, like the others of the house, was executed by plasterers from the London workshop of Joseph Rose, whom Adam had employed for many of his finest *décors*, including Nostell, Syon and Harewood. The walls are lined with grey scagliola Corinthian pilasters, worked by Bartoli, the capitals for which were sent over from London by Rose. Perhaps the most outstanding features are the magnificent curved mahogany doors which are inlaid with satin-wood and hung on pivots. Preston's splendid gilt furniture, mirrors and set of curtains supplied between 1815 and 1821 blend superbly with Wyatt's scheme and give the room a continental Empire atmosphere.

Flanking the saloon are the elegant dining- and drawing-rooms which interconnect to form an enfilade, or cross axis. The decoration of the dining-room seems to have changed little since Wyatt's day and still contains much of the furniture he designed, though the table was supplied by Preston. The drawing-room was entirely furnished and decorated by Preston and has been restored by the National Trust to its regency appearance. The doorcases are richly decorated in *pietro duro* as they are elsewhere, including the library where splendid bookcases made between 1792 and 1793, by the joiners Peacock and Berry, feature reeded mouldings and ribbon bandings in the uprights, a fluted architrave and guilloche dado. The chimney-piece of statuary marble, carved to simulate festooned drapery, is the finest of six mantels acquired at great expense from Westmacott of London in 1796, while Preston's curtains and valance were replaced in 1857 with the present 'figured crimson silk poplin' supplied by Gibson and Son.

The stone staircase rising from the hall between the

library and drawing-room is an adoption of an effective double-flight form used by Wyatt at Heaton. It leads up to a two-storey bedroom lobby – a distinctly Irish feature that is probably a legacy of Johnson's original plan; lit by an oval oculus it is surrounded at attic level by a colonnade inspired by the interior of the Parthenon and the temple of Poseidon at Paestum. Flanking the lobby is the boudoir which was used by the women of the house for sewing, reading, talking and playing the piano. This is an intimate and particularly attractive room whose original early nineteenth-century wallpaper, curtains, draperies and valance have been faithfully reproduced by the National Trust in 1980. Opposite lies the sumptuous state bedroom with its magnificent canopied bed and flame silk hangings supplied by Preston in anticipation of a visit by King George IV in 1821. Closed for over four years, this room is happily once again on public view and is one of the wonders of Castle Coole.

The National Trust acquired the house in 1951 and between 1980 and 1991 spent over four million pounds restoring the building and redecorating the interior. Though the present Earl of Belmore and his family still use Castle Coole, their principal residence is an elegant new house sited in the walled garden. It is said that the grey-lag geese, which have been at Castle Coole since 1700, will only go when the Belmores do. Except for some hardship during Hurricane Debbie in 1961, the flock has never shown any desire to leave, and the geese remain a wonderful sight on the lake.

Located just south east of Enniskillen on the main Belfast–Enniskillen Road (A4). NGR: H 260430. Open April, May and September: Saturdays, Sundays and bank holidays, 2.00 – 6.00 pm. Open daily during Easter: 2.00 – 6.00 pm. Open daily from June to August, except Thursdays: 2.00 – 6.00 pm. Grounds open from dawn to dusk all year. Toilet facilities. Admission to house: adults £2.30; children £1.15; groups £1.80. Admission to estate: £1.00 per car. Tel: (0365) 322690.

FLORENCE COURT

County Fermanagh

Few country houses can rival the wildly romantic parkland setting of Florence Court or its irresistibly attractive golden-grey façade, whose baroque composition of rustications, balustrades, pedimented niches, lugged surrounds and deep-set quoins has an ethereal, almost bucolic quality. The architect and date are unknown, as is so often the case in Ireland, but it was probably built around 1750 for John Cole, Baron Mount Florence, while the flanking arcades and pavilions were completed in 1771 for his son William Cole, first Earl of Enniskillen.

The original house at Florence Court was begun around 1718 by Sir John Cole (1680–1726), whose ancestors came from Devonshire during the reign of Queen Elizabeth and lived at Enniskillen Castle until it was burnt in 1710. Cole's 'very costly and sumptuous building', which he named after his wife Florence Wrey, was built in what was then 'a majestic wildness ... so wild that it was scarce inhabited by any human creatures but ye O's and Mac's, who ranged through the woods like so many freebooters pillaging all that came in their way'.

The building's early appearance is conjectural, but its basement was evidently retained for the present house, which was erected some time during the 1750s by the first Cole's son, John Cole – the first Lord Mount Florence (1709–67). His tall three-storey seven-bay block, which appears to have been built in two stages and completed by 1764, has a heavily enriched front façade, while the sides and back are plain by comparison – a characteristic feature of eighteenth-century Irish houses. In 1767 work began on the straight arcades and pavilions, which were later completed by William Willoughby Cole (1736–1803), created Earl of Enniskillen in 1776. These Palladian extensions, attributed to the Sardinian-born architect Davis Ducart, are more refined in detail and execution than the main block and were built as an integral part of a much larger architectural ensemble to the rear, comprising the yards, curved sweeps and crescent lawn. Once completed, the house was given an appropriate Brownian parkland setting between 1778 and 1780 by William King, probably the head gardener at the time, replacing straight tree-lined avenues and other features of a formal layout that had been created in the 1720s.

The vigorous baroque treatment of the exterior is

The dining-room in Florence Court

echoed in the large stone flagged hall with its triglyph frieze, banded pilasters, pedimented doorcase, massive Doric sandstone chimney-piece and linen-swag panels. The strong architectural character of this room is repeated in the adjacent library where the walls are lined with finely moulded pinewood bookcases, now filled with volumes on loan from Springhill. On the opposite side of the hall lies the service staircase and beyond this the study, whose high coved ceiling is decorated with a rather primitive rococo design of palmettes entwined with swirling scrolls. This room has only recently been opened to the public and contains an important Irish mahogany writing cabinet circa 1730 with a swan-neck pediment and grotesque mask on the frieze.

The large segmental arch at the rear of the hall, which opens onto the magnificent grand staircase, once had a partition wall and double doorcase, but in 1955 this was removed in the mistaken belief that it was a nineteenth-century addition. In fact, this arch was probably blocked around 1760 when the rear of the house was remodelled, as a result of which the staircase hall and its flanking drawing-room and dining-room are quite different in scale and mood from the front of the house. They are bright, large and well proportioned, with splayed windows, simple architraves and vigorous rococo plasterwork in the style of Robert West. Great panels of swirling foliage decorate the walls of the staircase hall with a Gothick cornice of cusped and ogee arches. Sadly, the elaborate drawing-room ceiling was lost in the fire of 1955, but the ceiling in the dining-room survives and is one of the best examples of rococo plasterwork outside of Dublin. It is composed of symmetrically arranged and naturally rendered scrolls of foliage, birds, rocaille work, shells and flamboyant palmiers. The centre-piece is an oval panel containing an eagle in high relief representing Zeus, who holds his thunderbolt and hovers in the midst of a stormy empyrean, surrounded by the heads of four cherubs virgorously puffing the winds to the four corners of the earth.

Visitors who look closely at the dining-room ceiling will notice some of the small holes drilled during the 1955 fire to allow the water pumped into the room above to drain away. These holes were the result of quick thinking on the part of the late Duchess of Westminster, Viola Grosvenor, who arrived during the fire to find little urgency about saving family treasures and discovered the old butler on the stairs removing a pair of his master's socks. She managed to get the servants to form a human chain and thus saved much of the house's contents. Unfortunately, the fire destroyed the fine plasterwork of the bedroom landing lantern, the martial decorations of the schoolroom ceiling and the Chinese wallpaper in the red room, while the grand staircase with its wonderful joinery was miraculously only slightly damaged. The plasterwork ceilings in the Venetian room and the entrance hall, which had been completely destroyed, were later expertly restored by the late Sir Albert Richardson.

The National Trust acquired Florence Court as a gift in 1954 from John Henry Cole, fifth Earl of Enniskillen (1876–1963). The contents and most of the land remained in the family and were subsequently inherited by his nephew David Lowry Cole, sixth Earl of Enniskillen (1918–89). The sixth Earl and his unpopular American wife left Florence Court for Scotland in January 1974, sadly leaving behind an empty house. The Trust has since successfully refur-

Grand staircase hall in Florence Court

nished the building through purchase, donations and bequests. The emphasis has been on acquiring eighteenth-century Irish furniture – an admirable policy considering the quintessentially Irish character of this endearing house.

Located 8 miles south west of Enniskillen on the Swanlinbar Road (A4). NGR: H 175343. Open April, May and September: Saturdays, Sundays and bank holidays, 1.00 – 6.00 pm. Open daily during Easter: 1.00 – 6.00 pm. Open daily from June to August, except Tuesdays: 1.00 – 6.00 pm. Gift shop and tea room open as house. Toilet facilities. Admission to house: adults £2.30; children £1.15; groups £1.80. Admission to estate: £1.00 per car. Tel: (036582) 249.

KYLEMORE ABBEY

County Galway

Kylemore Abbey is an intensely romantic place, an enchanted fairy-tale castle in the neo-Gothic style that stands dramatically at the foot of a barren mountain in a remote and beautiful part of Connemara – its numerous battlemented and machicolated towers and turrets reflected in the waters of the lake below. For years this amazing house, now a convent, has been the most admired and photographed building in the West of Ireland.

The castle was built between 1863 and 1868 for Mitchell Henry (1826–1911), a highly successful Manchester financier and MP, to the design of James Franklin Fuller and Ussher Roberts, brother of Field Marshal Roberts. The story of its building began in 1852 when Henry was on honeymoon with his bride Margaret Vaughan of Quilly House, County Down. Stopping near Kylemore Pass for an *al fresco* lunch, the young Mrs Henry looked up and saw a small shooting-box on the opposite hillside, the only dwelling in sight, and exclaimed: 'How I would love to live there.' Ten years later, Mitchell Henry, by now a rich tycoon, purchased the property with its 9,000 acres of moorland, mountain and lake and embarked upon a dream house for his wife.

The building took five years and cost over one and a quarter million pounds – a staggering sum in those days. The completed castle was on a 'Citizen Kane' scale, boasting many splendid reception rooms including a ball-room with a sprung floor, a magnificent staircase, a library, a study and thirty-three bedrooms. There were only four bathrooms, but the house was equipped with a Turkish bath, its water pressure ensured by an elaborate system of hydrants. He also built a model farm, laundry, dairy, saw mill, ornate chapel and a Gothic church, which was in part a replica of Norwich Cathedral. There was a six-acre walled garden and thanks to three miles of hot-water piping, twenty-one greenhouses containing tropical fruit, vineries, peaches, pineries and orangeries. Three hundred thousand trees were planted a year to protect the castle and gardens from constant gales and many of these grew successfully despite the harsh weather conditions.

For ten years the Henrys and their nine children lived at Kylemore, entertaining on a lavish scale. Tragedy struck in 1875 when Margaret died on a visit to Egypt. She was buried in a mausoleum at Kylemore, but afterwards her husband could no longer bear to spend much time there. Later his daughter Geraldine was killed when driving a pony-trap at Derryinver and shortly afterwards Henry's financial empire started to collapse. In 1902 Kylemore was acquired for a twentieth of its value by Mr Zimmerman, a Chicago businessman, as a present for his daughter who had married the Duke of Manchester. During their tenure from 1902 to 1913, when the estate was mortgaged to money lenders, they made many unfortunate changes, including transforming the lovely ball-room into an enormous kitchen. This conversion was undertaken to satisfy the cook who was expecting to prepare a meal for Edward VII and Queen Alexander on their visit to Connemara in 1903. Their Majesties did, in fact, come – but only for a cup of tea.

The old ball-room is now the chapel of the Irish Dames of Ypres who acquired Kylemore in 1920. This Benedictine congregation was founded originally in 1572 and later established by Dame Lucy Knatchbull at Ypres in 1665. They came to Ireland after their abbey was destroyed during the Great War and settled at Kylemore, where they established a famous girl's school.

Located between Letterfrack and Recess on the N59. NGR: L 748585. Open daily, 17 March to 31 October: 10.00 am – 6.00 pm. Closed Good Friday. Restaurant, craft shop and pottery shop as abbey. Toilet facilities. Admission to interpretative rooms: IR £1.00 p.p.; groups IR £0.75 p.p. Proceeds to restoration fund. Tel: abbey (095) 41146, shop (095) 41113.

MUCKROSS HOUSE

County Kerry

Muckross House is best known for its magical parkland setting beside the Lower Lake at Killarney, but the house is also worthy of its location. It was built between 1839 and 1843 for Colonel Henry Herbert to a design by the great Scottish architect William Burn, who was just beginning to establish himself as the most influential country house architect of his generation. Burn's brilliance lay principally in his ability to produce comfortable, well-organised houses, but Muckross is also a highly successful example of the Elizabethan Revival style, then very popular in Ireland. Its great array of tall chimneys, oriels, stepped gables, finials and mullioned windows are all skilfully integrated into a crisp, uncluttered composition that gains much from being faced with lavish quantities of silvery-pale Portland stone, shipped at great expense from Dorset and hauled by cart over the mountains from Kenmare.

Visitors enter the building through a *porte cochère* added by the Cork architect William Atkins around 1870. The interior was built with the same magnificence of the exterior, though sadly the rooms have now lost most of their original Victorian furnishings. Major H. A. Herbert, whose family had lived at Muckross since the early eighteenth century, was forced to sell the property in 1899 after he ran into serious financial difficulties. It was bought by Lord Ardilaun, a member of the Guinness family, and sold again in 1910 to William Bourn, a rich American gold miner who gave the house as a wedding present to his daughter Maud and her husband Arthur Vincent. Maud died of pneumonia in 1929 and three years later her husband bestowed Muckross together with the 11,000-acre estate upon the nation on the understanding that its peace and tranquillity would never be disturbed by the sound of motor cars.

The entrance hall is presided over by an impressive set of antlers of the long-extinct Irish elk – an inevitable status symbol of all large Irish country houses. From here visitors will find themselves channelled into the old billiard room with its display panels, rather than led directly into the main hall as the architect had intended. With its massive oak staircase lit by a window of English crystal, the main hall is a spacious room that serves as a focus for the whole house. In addition to an array of stags heads and portraits of the Vincent family, it contains two rather ponderous matching sideboards

The exterior of Muckross House

decorated with some fine woodcarving, made by the Egan family of Killarney.

In common with most houses of that period the main hall is flanked by the principal reception rooms along the garden front. All have fretted ceilings and immense bay windows which allow for marvellous views across sweeping lawns to the lake and mountains beyond. The drawing-room at the north end features a copy of a portrait of the long-lived Countess of Desmond, portraits of Maud Vincent and her husband by John Sargent, a pair of attractive Venetian mirrors and a locally made late nineteenth-century games table inlaid with mother-of-pearl. Passing through the library or saloon visitors will enter the dining-room – the only room in the house that really retains its authentic country house atmosphere. A good mahogany dining-room table with a set of twelve Chippendale chairs occupies the centre of the room, while at one end stands a large walnut sideboard carved in Italy and bearing the Herbert crest. This crest and the family motto 'Every man to his taste' are also found on the few surviving pieces of the Herbert dinner service on show here. The curtains, fragile and still quite beautiful, are original to this room and were woven in Brussels specifically for the visit of Queen Victoria and Prince Albert to Muckross in 1861.

On the first floor of the upper landing a few bedrooms, dressing rooms and children's rooms are open to the public. The main bedroom has a large Sheraton wardrobe and bed, while the pretty children's bedroom contains miniature furniture and toys. The

51

basement still features its old wine cellar, dairy, boiler room, kitchen and laundry, while the remaining rooms are used as regional craft workshops with working displays of book-binding, printing, wood-carving, harness-making, weaving, stonecutting, carpentry, shoe-making, basketry and pottery-making. There is also a blacksmith's forge and a representation of an early public house. The products of these workshops are sold at a craft shop in the old stables, where a large tea room overlooks the cobbled yard.

Located 3 miles south of Killarney on the Kenmare Road. NGR: V 965850. Open daily, July and August: 9.00 am – 7.00 pm. March to 30 June, September and October: 9.00 am – 6.00 pm. November to March: 9.00 am – 5.00 pm. Restaurant and craft shop. Tours by jaunting car or taxi tours from Killarney by arrangement. Extensive gardens and parkland open to public as house. Toilet facilities. Admission: adults IR £3.00; senior citizens IR £2.00; students and children IR £1.25; groups IR £2.00; family ticket IR £7.50. Tel: (064) 31440.

CASTLETOWN HOUSE

County Kildare

It may justly be said that Castletown is the largest and most splendid country house in Ireland, but it is also arguably the most important for it introduced sophisticated Palladianism from the continent and brought about a revolution in Irish architecture. The building was begun between 1721 and 1722 for William Conolly (1622–1729), the son of a Donegal innkeeper who, through astute dealings in forfeited estates after the Williamite wars, had become the richest man in Ireland. The house is an obvious manifestation of his wealth, but it also reflects the enormous political power that Conolly achieved following his election as Speaker of the Irish House of Commons in 1715 and his appointment as Lord Justice in 1716. Proud of his Irish identity, he consistently used his power to promote Irish interests. It was Conolly who instigated building the Parliament House on College Green, the first of its kind in Europe. Undoubtedly there were similar patriotic and political motivations underlying the building of his house at Castletown.

The design of the house was entrusted to the Florentine Alessandro Galilei (1691–1737), best known for his work on the Lateran Basilica in Rome. Although Galilei returned to Italy in 1719 having spent only a few months in Ireland, work on the building designs did not materialise until a few years later. Building was evidently well underway in July 1722, but with Galilei in Italy it is not clear who was supervising the operation. In 1724, however, the project was taken over by the twenty-five-year-old Edward Lovett Pearce who had just returned from Italy where he was studying the work of Palladio. Pearce had been in close touch with Galilei in Italy (whom he already knew through Vanbrugh, his cousin) and possibly helped him transmit designs back to Conolly in Ireland. Building operations at Castletown continued after Conolly's death in 1729 but came to a halt in 1733 with the early death of Pearce, by now Surveyor General and the most outstanding architect of his generation.

It is not known precisely how much of Castletown is Galilei's work, but he was certainly responsible for devising the overall scheme of the centre block, which was flanked by colonnades to lower service pavilions in the manner of Palladio's villas in the Veneto – a concept that was completely new in Ireland and later became the prototype and inspiration for numerous houses. The classically correct and regimented main façades of the centre block, both of which are almost identical, have the character of an Italian Renaissance town palazzo and are clearly also Galilei's work; their beauty and serenity are enormously enhanced by the silvery-white limestone which, unlike other Irish limestones, is free from age-darkening and blackening from the rain. The pavilions, designed by Pearce, are composed of a coarser and less dazzling golden-brown limestone; together with the curved colonnades they have the effect of focussing the eye upon the centre block.

The interior plan of Castletown was probably largely devised by Pearce, although it incorporates some archaic features, such as the arrangement of rooms in an enfilade along the ground-floor garden front. Adhering to the seventeenth-century baroque tradition, these rooms meet in a central saloon and terminate with antechambers at each end. The saloon (now the green drawing-room) opens into the two-storey entrance hall, crossed along the inside wall by a corridor running through the central axis of the house. Another corridor directly above this is carried by a balustraded gallery supported by a screen of Ionic columns. It is a magnificent entrance hall – almost certainly designed by Pearce and the only large room that has survived intact from the Speaker's day. Pearce's device of a columnar screen at one end of the hall was later adopted by many Irish houses, such as Castle Ward in County Down. Another novel feature of the plan which subsequently entered the vocabulary of Irish country house architecture was the location of the main staircase in a separate chamber to the side of the hall. However, this chamber evidently remained without its staircase for forty years, as Speaker Conolly's widow preferred to leave the interior unfinished, though she continued to live at Castletown in great style until her death in 1752. She was, none-the-less, responsible for building work in the demesne, notably the Conolly Folly (1740), the Wonderful Barn (1743) and the Batty Langley Lodge (circa 1745).

Castletown's interior was largely created during the time of Tom Conolly, the Speaker's great nephew, who inherited the property in 1758 when he was twenty-four. That same year he married the fifteen-year-old Lady Louisa Lennox, daughter of the second Duke of Richmond, whose older sister Emily had already married James, the Earl of Kildare, and was living nearby at Carton. By all accounts Tom Conolly had a weak, indecisive character, but Louisa was extremely dynamic and immediately set about completing the house.

The staircase hall was Louisa's first objective. She employed the Dutch-Italian sculptor and stonemason Simon Vierpyl to install the magnificent Portland-stone cantilevered staircase in 1760; the unusual brass balustrade in the form of Doric columns is signed 'A. King Dublin 1760'. As substantial payments were made to the famous Swiss-Italian stuccodores – the Francini brothers – in 1765 it may be assumed that the plasterwork in the staircase hall was applied then, except for the cornice and coffered ceiling which belong to Pearce's time. The Francini brothers first came to Ireland in 1739 and are credited with the introduction of human figures into plaster decoration; characteristically, their plasterwork on the staircase incorporates a number of family portraits as well as large canvases, notably 'The Boar Hunt' by Snyders.

Alterations and improvements to the house during the period of 1760 to 1766 included the creation of the dining-room and work on the red and green drawing-rooms. On stylistic grounds it has been maintained that these rooms, which feature ceilings of Jonesian-inspired geometrical plasterwork, were designed by Sir William Chambers – an argument supported by the fact that Simon Vierpyl was one of his protégés and may have supervised the work since Chambers never actually came to Ireland. The dining-room to the left of the hall was created by throwing together two earlier rooms, while at the same time the ground-floor windows were lowered twenty-one inches. It was in the dining-room that legend has it Tom Conolly entertained the devil, whom he had met out hunting and invited back, believing him to be a 'dark stranger' but realising the truth after his guest had removed his boots to reveal hairy feet shaped like cloven hooves. A priest was summoned in haste; he hurled his breviary at the devil, missed and cracked a mirror, whereupon the devil took fright and vanished up the chimney, leaving behind a split hearthstone and a cracked mirror to this day.

The green drawing-room, formerly the saloon, has been restored with green silk copied from the original fabric (1765) and gilded fillet copied from Chamber's design for the fillet in the gallery at Osterley Park. It contains a japanned lacquer cabinet that belonged to old Mrs Conolly and is inscribed 'Mrs Conolly to Miss Burten' with drawers painted with charming Italianate scenes. Flanking the door are portraits of Speaker Conolly and his wife Katherine by Jervas. The adjacent print room was created by Lady Louisa Conolly between 1766 and 1768 with the help of her sister Sarah. The fashion for pasting engravings and mezzotints onto walls during the long winter days became very popular at that time. The print room at Castletown is possibly the earliest to survive – it is certainly the only one that still exists in Ireland. Used as the billiard room in the last century, it now contains Louis XVI furniture with Aesop's fables in tapestry, a gift to Castletown which looks very well here.

Apparently inspired by her success in the print room, Louisa Conolly decided to redecorate the long gallery – an eighty-foot-long room on the first floor directly above the garden front enfilade. She had the old plaster panels 'knocked off smack smooth' and Pompeian decoration painted onto the walls by two English artists, Charles Reuban Riley and Thomas Riley, between 1775 and 1777. Plans to remove the old Pearce ceiling and frieze were dropped and the ceiling was instead redecorated with colours matching the walls. The glass chandeliers from Murano near Venice were bought to match the room's colour, though Louisa was disappointed when they arrived, claiming they were the wrong blue. Four doors once led into the room but after remodelling there was only one entrance, although another blind door had been created to disguise the fact that the landing entrance was placed off centre. The lunette above the doors is copied from Guido Reni's 'Aurora', while the portrait of Tom Conolly over the mantelpiece at the end of the room was painted in 1758 by Mengs in Rome. A visitor in 1778 found the room furnished 'in the most delightful manner with fine glasses, books, musical instruments, billiard table – in short, everything that you can think of . . . and though so large it is so well fitted that it is the warmest, most comfortable looking place I ever saw and they tell me they live in it quite in the winter, for the servants can bring in dinners at one end without anyone hearing at the other.'

Tom Conolly died in 1803 but Lady Louisa lived on for many years. She eventually died in 1821, seated in a tent erected on the lawn in front of Castletown, for it was her wish that she should go looking at the house she had loved so much. The house then passed to the grandson of Tom Conolly's sister Harriett, Colonel Edward Michael Pakenham, who changed his name to Conolly. He was succeeded in 1848 by his son Thomas Conolly (1823–76), and later in turn by both of his sons. Upon the death of Major Conolly in 1956, Castletown was inherited by Lord Carew who put it up for auction in 1965. The land was bought by property speculators who proceeded to build a housing estate beside the 250-year-old lime avenue. Ultimately in 1967 the decaying house and 120 acres were bought in the eleventh hour by Desmond Guinness in order to save Castletown for posterity. It became the head-quarters of the Irish Georgian Society, who with the help of weekend volunteers and money raised at home and abroad managed to repair the building and refurnish some of the rooms. In 1992 it was acquired by the Office of Public Works and its future is now finally assured, although the battle to recover its dispersed contents may be waged for generations to come.

Located 1 mile north east of Celbridge. NGR: N 980342.
Open April to September: Mondays to Fridays, 10.00 am –
6.00 pm; Saturdays, 11.00 am – 6.00 pm; Sundays and
bank holidays, 2.00 – 6.00 pm. October: Mondays to
Fridays, 10.00 am – 5.00 pm; Sundays and bank holidays,
2.00 – 5.00 pm. November to March: Sundays and bank
holidays, 2.00 – 5.00 pm. Refreshments available. Toilet
facilities. Admission: adults IR £2.50; senior citizens and
students IR £2.00; family IR £6.00. Tel: (01) 6288252.

KILKENNY CASTLE

County Kilkenny

The imposing ancestral castle of the Ormonde Butlers
stands in the south-east corner of the medieval city of
Kilkenny in a magnificent location over the River Nore.
Largely the creation of local architect William Robertson in the 1820s, the building owes more to the spirit
of romance than to historical accuracy. None-the-less,
it retains portions of earlier buildings, including the
basic plan and shape of the great medieval fortress – a
castle that has served as a princely residence for over
eight centuries and played a major role in the country's
history.

It appears that a motte (a Norman fortification dug
out of earth) was first erected here by Richard de Clare
(Strongbow) as early as 1172, but this structure,
destroyed by Donald O'Brien, King of Thomond, was
rebuilt during 1207 and 1213 by Strongbow's son-in-
law and successor, William Marshall, Earl of Pembroke. As befitting a potentate of enormous wealth and
power, the new castle was erected on an impressive
scale. At each angle of a trapezoid enclosure were
massive drum towers, three of which still survive in an
altered form together with the original north wall. The
castle remained intact until the mid seventeenth
century, by which time it had become the principal seat
of the powerful Butler family – purchased by James
Butler, third Earl of Ormonde, from the Earl Marshall's
descendants in 1391. After the Restoration in 1660, the
Great Duke of Ormonde, inspired by buildings he had
seen in France during his exile, carried out a major

rebuilding of the old castle which had been damaged during Cromwell's siege in 1650. The second Duke continued his father's work and was responsible for the classical-style entrance gateway on the street, built during 1703 and 1706; however, following his exile in 1715 for supporting the Jacobite cause, the castle lay empty until the estates devolved upon Walter Butler of Kilcash in 1766. Walter's son John was recognised as the seventeenth Earl of Ormonde in 1791 and shortly afterwards he built the extensive stables across the street – now the home of the Kilkenny Design Centre.

According to tradition, the nineteenth-century remodelling of the castle came about in 1826 when the Kilkenny architect William Robertson, who had been walking in the castle courtyard with Lady Ormonde, suddenly paused and pointed out that the main wall was out of alignment and consequently unsafe. This observation gave him the commission to rebuild the castle on a massive scale; as the Marquess of Ormonde was one of Ireland's richest landlords, no expense was spared. The building of sham castles was all the rage at the time, so it was hardly surprising that Robertson should have chosen to recreate the romantic appearance of the medieval castle. He duly swept away all of the first Duke's charming buildings, fortunately leaving the second Duke's classical gateway. The castle that emerged was externally a rather grim essay in neo-feudalism and internally distinguished only by its dullness. Subsequent alterations to the castle from 1859 to 1862 by Benjamin Woodward and his partner Thomas Deane improved the castle, though it was always the magnificent collection of tapestries, portraits, furniture and above all the famous Ormonde gold plate which redeemed the dark rooms of the interior. It was therefore a tragedy when the contents were sold in 1935, bringing to an end the centuries-old occupation of the castle. In 1967 the sixth Marquess gave the castle to a local preservation society who two years later transferred it to the state to be restored and managed on behalf of the nation.

Extensive restoration began in 1973, but as yet only portions of the castle are open to the public. This includes the hall, which retains its fine eighteenth-century black-and-white flagged floor, and walls that were once covered with gilded Spanish leather, while its elaborate ceiling is a modern replica of the original. The great mahogany staircase brings the visitor to the dining-room, located in the circular north-east tower with its twelve-foot-thick walls; a further set of stairs winds upwards to a corridor leading to the principal restored room of the castle – the picture gallery. Occupying the entire length of the castle's east wing, it measures 150-feet long, twenty-seven-feet wide and thirty-feet high to the apex of the hammer-beamed roof. Between 1859 and 1862 Benjamin Woodward introduced a partly glazed roof so that this immense space could be lit, while John Hungerford Pollen painted the roof trusses in the pre-Raphaelite style. Pollen, one time professor of fine arts at University College, Dublin, was also responsible for the white Carrara marble double chimney-piece which he carved himself, complete with a series of *bas-reliefs* illustrating important events in the Butler family history. The walls of this room are again lined with pictures, and although these are but a few compared to the 184 paintings it once contained, some of the magic and grandeur of this room has now been restored, providing visitors with a fitting climax to a tour of this historic castle.

Located within the city of Kilkenny. NGR: S 509557. Open daily, June to September: 10.00 am – 7.00 pm. April and May: 10.00 am – 5.00 pm. October to March: Tuesdays to Saturdays, 10.30 am – 12.45 pm and 2.00 – 5.00 pm; Sundays, 11.00 am – 12.45 pm and 2.00 – 5.00 pm. Guided tours available. Art gallery in basement (collection of 19th- and 20th-century Irish paintings) along with restaurant. Parkland and gardens open daily from 10.00 am. Kilkenny Design Centre located in the castle stables opposite the main entrance. Toilet facilities. Admission: adults IR £1.00; senior citizens IR £0.70; students and children IR £0.40; groups IR £0.70; family ticket IR £3.00. Tel: (056) 21450.

EMO COURT

County Leix

The spectacular mansion of Emo Court, with its fine garden and parkland setting, is perhaps best known as James Gandon's sole venture into the field of monumental domestic architecture. It was designed around 1790 on the same magnificent scale as his Custom House (1781–91) and Four Courts (1786) and in common with these was built in the neo-classical style – the style in which Gandon had established himself as the pre-eminent architect of late eighteenth-century

Ireland.

The house was commissioned by John Dawson, Viscount Carlow and the first Earl of Portarlington – a man of undoubted architectural knowledge who was instrumental in bringing Gandon to Ireland. Dawson engaged Gandon primarily to design the nearby church at Coolbanagher (1782–83); later he requested plans for a new county seat to replace Dawson Court, built by his grandfather Ephraim Dawson in the early eighteenth century. A new site was chosen for the house which was named Emo – an Italianised version of Imoe, the original Irish name of the demesne. As designed by Gandon, it has a giant pedimented Ionic portico dominating the centre of the entrance front, flanked by two end pavilions making it in all a nine-bay composition with two storeys over a basement. Panels containing Coadstone reliefs of putti representing the Arts and a pastoral scene, dated 1794, crown the blind attics of the pavilions.

Sadly, Gandon's building was never completed as Lord Portarlington died of an illness when out campaigning during the 1798 rebellion. Despite their motto 'Virtue is the Way of Life', the family fortune was subsequently dissipated through gambling and the second Earl was unable to finance further building until 1834 when he employed the English architect Lewis Vulliamy, assisted by Arthur and John Williamson of Dublin, to make improvements. They worked on the interior as well as completing the garden front, giving it a portico of four tall Ionic columns with a balustraded entablature to complement Gandon's front elevation. Finally in 1861, after the Encumbered Estates Court came close to ordering a compulsory sale of the estate, the third Earl somehow found enough money to build the great rotunda, whose copper-clad dome rising from behind the garden front was designed by William Caldbeck of Dublin. The mile-long Wellingtonia avenue was planted at this time and formal gardens laid out around the house.

The Portarlingtons sold Emo in 1930 to the Society of Jesus for use as a seminary. In 1969 the property was bought from the Jesuits by C. D. Cholmeley-Harrison of Woodstown House in County Waterford, who has subsequently carried out a magnificent restoration and refurbishment of the house upon the advice of the late Sir Albert Richardson's firm, a renowned specialist in the conservation of Georgian buildings.

Unfortunately, much of Gandon's interior at Emo failed to survive nineteenth-century alterations. An important exception is the entrance hall – an attractive single-storey room whose apsidal ends were painted with *trompe l'oeil* paintings in the 1970s to represent plaster decoration that Gandon had originally intended. The hall leads directly into Calbeck's great rotunda – a magnificent circular space lit by a lantern in a high coffered dome which rests on Siena-marble pilasters with richly gilded Corinthian capitals. A more successful room would be difficult to find in Ireland, except perhaps for Johnson's amazing staircase rotunda at Townley Hall.

The rotunda is flanked by the dining-room on one side and the library, formerly the anteroom, on the other. Both rooms have handsome plasterwork ceilings designed by Vulliamy – that in the library has gold-painted rococo decoration which matches the room's remarkable chimney-piece, an enormous white marble monstrosity packed with playful putti and an excess of grapes. From the present library the visitor enters the old library, now the drawing-room – an enormous room that extends the entire way down from the front to the back of the house. It is divided by screens of Connemara marble columns, has distempered apple-green walls and extends into a wide curving bow in the centre of one of the long sides. Some fine pictures hang in this room, notably a large canvas over the mantel-piece of 'Christ and the Woman of Samaria at the Well' by Francesco Trevisani, together with paintings by Abraham Bisschop, Lemaire Poussin and the Irishman James Arthur O'Connor. There is also a fine mid eighteenth-century Irish mahogany settee and a good collection of ceramics including a delicately adorned little Meissen tray.

The restoration of Emo did not end with the house. Mr Cholmeley-Harrison has also admirably restored the gardens, planting many new trees and shrubs. In an area of the demesne park now owned by the Forest Commission stands the ruin of a building known as the Temple – a remarkable gazebo built around 1760 on alignment with Dawson's Court. It consists of a triumphal arch surmounted by an octagonal two-storied turret that was formerly domed. No doubt it was used for entertaining as it had a kitchen in the basement. A short distance away on Spike Hill is an obelisk.

Located 6 miles south of Portlaoise. NGR: N 539066.
Open Mondays between 15 March and 18 October: 2.00 –
6.00 pm; other times by appointment. Garden open daily:
10.30 am – 5.30 pm. Tea, scones and cake available in the
old pump house. Toilet facilities. Admission: adults IR
£2.50; senior citizens, students and children IR £1.00;
combined ticket for house and garden IR £3.50. Tel:
(0502) 26110.

GLIN CASTLE

County Limerick

The late Georgian gothicisation of Glin Castle is only
skin deep, but its pasteboard-like loops, crenellations
and gleaming white walls have an ethereal quality that
is particularly memorable. The castle's magic is further
enhanced by a serene parkland setting, delightful
gingerbread Gothick gatelodges and a lush location
facing across the Shannon Estuary. The romantically
titled Knights of Glin have retained ownership of their
lands here for seven centuries in spite of sharing a
familiar history of rebellion, attainders and confis-
cations with the other Desmond Geraldines.

Fragments of the old medieval castle of Glin can be
seen in the village and were built by one of the early
Knights, whose family – a cadet branch of the Fitz-
Geralds (the Earls of Desmond) – had held their rather
unusual title since the fourteenth century. The castle
was seriously damaged by the Lord President of
Munster, Sir George Carew, in 1600 and completely
destroyed following another siege in 1641. By the
century's end the family was living one mile west of the
old ancestral castle in a thatched house known as Glin
Hall. They remained true to the old faith until Edward,
the twentieth Knight, conformed to Protestantism in
1737. Although he died soon thereafter as a result of
dancing at his wedding feast, his three younger brothers
became adherents of the Anglican faith as they succeeded to the title: Edmund who died in 1763, Richard
the duellist who died in 1775, and Thomas who died in
1781. They all continued to live at Glin Hall, though
the castle was rebuilt in a grander fashion after a fire in
1740.

It was Thomas's son – Colonel John Bateman Fitz-
Gerald, the twenty-fourth Knight – who began con-

structing the present mansion on the site of Glin Hall shortly after his marriage in 1789. The new house was designed as a plain three-storey double-bow fronted building with a long service wing, but due to financial problems the third floor was not completed by the time of his death in 1803. His son John Fraunceis Fitz-Gerald, following the fashion of the time, added battlements and turrets after his marriage in 1812 and rechristened it Glin Castle. He liked gambling and evidently was rather successful for he laid out much of the present park, built a hermitage made of tufa, a Gothic folly, the demesne wall (erected as a result of a bet with a local landlord) and three delightful castellated entrances to the demesne, one of which was a copy of the second family crest – 'a castle of two towers argent'.

The interior is noted for its very fine neo-classical plasterwork and above all for its magnificent Irish furniture, much of which has been collected over the past two decades by Desmond Fitz-Gerald, the present Knight of Glin. It also has many interesting family portraits; a few of the finest hang in the great hall – a splendid room divided by a ceiling in the Adam manner which keeps its original colouring. Over the sandstone chimney-piece hangs Joseph Wilson's portrait of the builder of the house, John Bateman Fitz-Gerald, dressed in his uniform as Colonel of the Royal Glin Artillery and dated around 1780. On one of the side walls, above a grotesque blackened mahogany side-table with the family coat of arms, is a full-length portrait by Highmore (circa 1745) of Richard Fitz-Gerald, the duellist Knight, being challenged to a duel. Always willing to engage in personal combat, Richard offered his opponents the choice between pistols at twenty paces or the short sword wielded within a ten-foot ring – an unpleasant prospect as he was an accomplished swordsman and an excellent shot. On one occasion when engaged in a duel with a Spaniard, Richard was unable to drive his sword home until his servant cried out: 'Stick him where they stick the pigs', whereupon the Spaniard was pierced through the throat and was found later to have been wearing protective chain mail under his clothing.

The great hall opens through two fanlighted door-ways at the far end into the inner hall, where a most unusual flying staircase springs first on two ramps and then rises on a central flight to the gallery above. It is lit by a Venetian window overlooking the formal garden which is surmounted by an elliptical relieving arch with delicate cornucopia and plaster flowers in the spandrels. The plasterwork in the drawing-room is similar though less refined than in the hall, with fruit and flowers and a radiating fan design as the centre-piece. The room has a superb inlaid chimney-piece by Bossi circa 1790 whose marble colouring matches the frame of the portrait above depicting Selina Blennerhassett, the only female member of the notorious Limerick Hell Fire Club. In the adjacent library a tall mahogany bookcase features a broken pediment surmounted by a bust of Milton, with brass grilles in four oval openings; one conceals a hidden door leading to the staircase. The room also contains a very fine Irish eighteenth-century library cabinet with an adjustable reading top and swan-pedimented bookcase, while over the mantelpiece hangs a mirror dating from 1760 and made by the great craftsmen Francis and John Booker of Dublin.

In sharp contrast to other Irish country houses, there is no doubt that Glin Castle looks better today than it has ever done in the past. Aside from being completely restored in recent decades, it has become home to many fine examples of Irish furnishings collected by the present Knight as part of his efforts to ensure that the finest examples of eighteenth- and nineteenth-century Irish craftsmanship remain in Ireland. Desmond Fitz-Gerald, who is the twenty-ninth holder of the title, is Christie's representative in Ireland and is well known and respected for his outstanding contribution to the study of Irish furniture, paintings, architecture and historic gardens.

Located 1 mile west of Glin village. NGR: R 123472. Open daily during May: 10.00 am – 12.00 pm and 2.00 – 4.00 pm; other times by appointment. Dinners and lunches provided for groups by appointment; contact Madam Fitz-Gerald at (068) 34173 or Mrs O'Sullivan at (068) 36230. Toilet facilities. Admission: adults IR £2.00; senior citizens IR £1.50; students and children IR £0.50; groups IR £1.50.

Glin Castle and gardens

SPRINGHILL

County L'Derry

Considering the harsh and unappealing conditions that still prevailed in late seventeenth-century Ulster, it is perhaps surprising that country seats developing at that time were often pleasant and unassuming buildings exuding a feeling of warmth. Sadly, such houses from this period are now rare, though one particularly attractive and well-preserved example is Springhill – a charming and almost timeless building whose white-washed front façade still brings to mind 'something of the ancient dignity of resident landlords' as it did for Sampson, writing nearly two centuries ago.

The early history of Springhill is a little elusive, but the present house was built by William 'Good-Will' Conyngham as part of his marriage contract to Anne Upton in 1680 to 'erect a convenient dwelling house of lime and stone, two stories high, with necessary office houses, gardens and orchards'. It is not known if a dwelling stood here previously, but the townland of Ballindrum (Springhill) had been bought for £200 by Good-Will Conyngham's father in 1658. Earlier it belonged to a London company, the Salters, and prior to this had formed part of the ancient territory of the O'Cahan's.

Although enlarged with wide canted-bay pavilions in the late eighteenth-century, the house that Good-Will built survives much as he left it – a gable-ended block of two storeys over a basement with a steeply pitched roof, solid brick chimneys at each end and tall, thin windows in a seven-bay symmetrical front façade. Springhill faces north onto a deep courtyard flanked by long, low office ranges with pointed windows (a later insertion) and curvilinear 'Holborn gables' – a Flemish type which seems to have been much used in late seventeenth-century Ulster. Front courtyards were a standard feature of the period and Springhill was originally entered from the north through large gates aligned upon a long, straight avenue. The main out-buildings, grouped around a series of small yards flanking the house, include a recently restored barn with pistol loops and an important oak roof, which like that of the main house incorporated butt purloins, rare in Ireland. Tree-ring dating by Queen's University, Belfast, revealed a date of 1694 for a lintel from this barn, while a floor joist timber from the attic of the main house produced a felling date of 1697.

The seventeenth-century building has a tripartite

Rear view of Springhill

plan with a centrally placed stair projection at the back. Approached by four stone steps leading to a door with a plain stone frame, it reveals a square entrance hall with bold bolection plaster panelling that is probably contemporary with the house. The door to the staircase hall is flanked by two pikes used in the Battle of Vinegar Hill, County Wexford, during the 1798 rebellion. This magnificent broad staircase is the real glory of Springhill and one of the earliest to survive in Ireland. The treads are made of oak while the handrail and balusters – alternately plain and spiral twisted – are made from yew. Ancestral portraits line the walls above, including one of Good-Will Conyngham, while at the foot of the stairs is a heavy oak chest inscribed 'John Smith maid this in 1714'.

To the left of the entrance hall lies the gun room, a dark, masculine room which retains its original bolection moulded oak panelling. Formerly the dining-room, it must have been made into a small drawing-room around 1770 as restoration work during the 1960s accidentally revealed pretty handprinted English wallpaper in the panel frames. Later it became home to a fine collection of guns and swords reflecting the family's military past. Among the items on display are a few bulky blunderbusses, a Kentucky rifle, duelling pistols and a number of flintlocks, later converted to muzzleloaders and used in the siege of Derry in 1689.

The library on the opposite side of the hall houses an outstanding collection of books, most of which were acquired by Colonel William Conyngham (1723–84). Opposite the fireplace is a fine library cabinet whose double-arched top dates from the late seventeenth century, while a fascinating medicine chest full of drawers and bottles stands beside the drawing-room door; originally belonging to the Duke of Marlborough, he gave it to his aide-de-camp, the third Viscount Molesworth, after he saved his life during the Battle of Ramillies in 1706. The set of heavy chairs in the room are early nineteenth-century copies of Jacobean originals; according to family history, the original chairs were destroyed by Olivia, second wife of George Lennox-Conyngham (1752–1816). One chair was spared, however, and Maxwell, the estate carpenter, remade the lot.

The large and lofty drawing-room, added by Colonel William Conyngham sometime after he inherited the property in 1765, creates a striking contrast to the small rooms of the original house. French Empire sofas, Louis XV tables and an armchair, a Dutch rosewood cabinet and a circular mahogany inlaid regency table grace the scene, while family portraits by Hugh Douglas Hamilton, William Hoare and Pompeo Batoni hang on the walls. There is also a pretty portrait of Harriet Molesworth by Sir Francis Cotes. The unfortunate Harriet lost her leg while trying to escape a fire at her London home, and an ivory walking stick presented to her by King George III is displayed on a small Chinese cupboard beneath her portrait.

Next to the drawing-room and overlooking the park is the dining-room, added by William, 'Wims', Lenox-Conyngham (1792-1858) shortly after his marriage in 1819. It has red flock wallpaper, a set of marquetry walnut fiddle-back chairs of the William and Mary period (circa 1700) and a chimney-piece of yellow marble brought from Herculaneum by the eccentric Earl Bishop of Derry and presented by him to the family in the early 1780s. Over the chimney-piece hangs a still life of birds in the manner of Hondecoeter and on the opposite wall is the celebrated picture known as 'The Grand Tour Group', painted in Rome between 1772 and 1773 by Philip Wickstead. It depicts John Staples with Thomas Orde, Richard Neville, Sir

William Young and James Byres admiring an antique sculpture. The picture is appropriately flanked by portraits of John Staples's daughter Charlotte and her husband Wims Lenox-Conyngham.

Elsewhere in Springhill are many small rooms, old powder closets and even a secret staircase now permanently concealed. There are curious sloping alcoves for beds in the attics and below, on the first floor, a charming day nursery. One of the two bedrooms open to the public is the blue room where George Lenox-Conyngham shot himself in 1816 after spending many months 'in a melancholy state of mind'. His wife, Olivia, haunts the scene; her ghost is one of the most widely authenticated phantoms in Ulster.

Outside, in the old laundry yard, lies an important costume collection begun in 1964 with a loan from the Pack-Beresford family and subsequently expanded by the National Trust. It now contains over 2,300 items, including a Court Mantua made in England in 1759 and featuring brocaded Spitalfields silk. The collection is displayed in rotation each year.

Springhill was given as a gift to the National Trust in 1957 by Captain William Lenox-Conyngham shortly before his death. Included in the transfer was the magnificent 300-year-old beech avenue which sadly had to be replanted in 1984 after the trees developed beech bark disease.

Located near Moneymore on the Coagh Road (B18). NGR: H 869828. Open April, May, June and September: Saturdays, Sundays and bank holidays, 2.00 – 6.00 pm. Open daily during Easter: 2.00 – 6.00 pm. Open daily during July and August, except Thursdays: 2.00 – 6.00 pm. Gift shop and tea room open as house. Wheelchair access to all ground-floor rooms. Toilet facilities. Admission: adults £2.20; children £1.00; groups £1.60. Tel: (06487) 48210.

Carrigglas Manor

CARRIGGLAS MANOR

County Longford

The blue-grey limestone façade of Carrigglas, with its great oriel windows, battlemented turrets and high-pitched gables, has a mystical, almost dream-like quality as it rises serenely over the surrounding park-land. A finer example of castellated Tudor Revival architecture would be difficult to find. Carrigglas was designed by the Scottish architect Daniel Robertson in 1837 for Thomas Langlois Lefroy, Lord Chief Justice of Ireland, replacing an earlier house belonging to Lord Newcomen who had committed suicide after his bank collapsed. The Lefroy family still live in and maintain the house. With most of its original pictures, artefacts and furniture still intact, the interior exudes an atmosphere of early Victorian living that is unspoiled by later decorative schemes.

Passing through a formal entrance hall revealing hard wooden seats for unwanted guests, one arrives in a central chamber dominated by a staircase notable for its cast-iron handrails. This room is lit by a stained-glass window displaying the Lefroy coat of arms. (The Lefroys are a family of French Huguenot ancestry. The first member to settle in Ireland was Thomas's father, the family having previously been silk dyers in England and bankers in Laverno, Italy.) Below the window stands a bust of Thomas – or the Chief, as he was called – modelling as a Roman senator. An enigmatic and colourful character, he had in his youth become an *inamorato* of Jane Austen and was later immortalised as Darcy in *Pride and Prejudice*.

Magnificent double doors with Gothic panelling link the three principal reception rooms in an enfilade along the garden front. At one end lies the drawing-room with its striking compartmented ceiling and cornice of foliage, still coloured the original hues of rose and pale blue. The furniture in this room largely came from Dutch relatives, while the splendid chimney-piece was a gift from Thomas's aunt, the Countess of Carrara, who sent over a block of white marble with a mason to carve it *in situ*. The adjacent library has a comfortable appearance; big arm chairs, a Siena fire-place, Tudor-Gothic doors and a Gothic bookcase create an air of ease and repose. Portraits of various ancestors gaze down from the walls, as they do in the dining-room where the walls still retain their original

stone colour. Despite its large size, the dining-room ha
quite a warm feel created by the mellow glow of th
mahogany table, the old Turkish carpet and the re
upholstered dining chairs. A magnificent Chines
painted leather screen stands close to the fireplace
while above the mantel a large portrait of Chief Justic
Lefroy commands all aspects of the room.

Upstairs the bedrooms seem endless. One room ha
a particularly fine silk oriental carpet, an enormou
four-poster bed, Irish rosewood table and Staffordshir
his-and-hers washing sets. The floral patterned wall
paper is copied from Queen Victoria's bedchamber a
Osbourne.

Visitors to Carrigglas must inspect the magnificen
double courtyard stable and farmyard complex tha
was erected before 1790 to the designs of Jame
Gandon, architect of the Custom House and Fou
Courts. Gandon also designed the main entrance to th
park, with their symmetrical flanking lodges.

Located 3 miles north east of Longford on the Granard
Road (T15/R194). NGR: N 170770. Open daily, 5 June to
5 September, except Tuesdays and Wednesdays: 1.00 –
5.00 pm (6.00 pm in August); Sundays, 2.00 – 6.00 pm.
Groups should book in advance. Lunch in house and tea
room. Dinner by special arrangement. Gift shop. Toilet
facilities. Admission to the house: adults IR £1.50; senior
citizens and children IR £1.00. Gardens extra. Accommodation in house and self-catering apartments in stableyard
available. Tel: (043) 45165.

BEAULIEU
County Louth

On the banks of the River Boyne, lying a few mile
upstream from Drogheda, stands Beaulieu, alias Bewle
– a house of considerable charm and enormou
architectural importance. It was built in the years c
peace and prosperity following the Restoration i
1660, when Irish landowners abandoned their medieva
castles and built unfortified luxurious seats. Almost a
known examples of these Carolinian country house
have now vanished and only the unchanged splendou
and refinement of Beaulieu survives to bear witness t
this major turning point in the development of Iris

architecture.

The house was built between 1661 and 1667 by Sir William Tichborne, who had been granted possession of the property by Charles II in 1662. His father, Sir Henry Tichborne, the prominent military commander in the Civil War, had resided as a tenant in the old castle at Beaulieu since 1650, having purchased the rights from the mortgagees – the Peppard brothers. From the thirteenth century, ownership of the castle, which stood north west of the present house, had belonged to the Plunkett family, but in 1639 it was mortgaged and in 1642 was forfeited by the Cromwellian regime in retaliation for William Plunkett's participation in the 1641 rebellion.

Externally the house has remained virtually unaltered since the 1660s, although until the nineteenth century it was surrounded by a twelve-foot-high protective hedge. Beaulieu is a seven-bay two-storied building and like many English houses of that time was built in the so-called 'artisan mannerist' style, with cantilevered eaves carried on a massive wooden modillion course and a dormered attic in a high-hipped roof surmounted by tall, symmetrical chimney stacks. The rendered walls are of stone, but delicately rubbed orange-pink bricks from Holland have been used for the window surrounds and the string coursing which firmly encloses the house. Any sense of monotony is broken by the grouping of windows on the side façades and by the pushing forward of the two end bays of the front elevation, whose angles are strengthened by stone quoins.

The interior still contains a great deal of its original fittings. The lofty two-storied hall, lit by first-floor windows, retains its arched doorways, cornice and large wooden chimney-piece and overmantel, the latter adorned with a painting of the town of Drogheda. Both the dining-room and drawing-room have kept their red pine panelling with bolection mouldings (a form of moulding which projects in front of the face of the frame) and their original ceilings with central ovals surrounded by heavy floral garlands. The ceiling in the drawing-room features a skewed-perspective painting attributed to Willem van der Hagen depicting a gallery opening into a clouded and cherubined sky.

Most of the subsequent alterations to the interior were undertaken in the early eighteenth century by the son of the builder of the house, Sir Henry Tichborne, the first and last Baron Ferrard (1663–1731) who succeeded to the property in 1693. His most important addition was the grand staircase with its finely carved balusters and ramps at the newels, installed between 1722 and 1723. Other alterations at this time included a corridor on the first-floor landing and elaborate woodcarvings added to the arches over the doors in the front hall. It is also likely that Tichborne was responsible for replacing the original mullioned and casement windows with their sash openings.

After Lord Ferrard's death from apoplexy in 1731 the house was inherited by his son-in-law, William Aston, MP; after 1769 it passed to William Aston's brother-in-law, Thomas Tipping, MP, from whom it devolved through the female line to the Montgomery family and the present owner, Mrs Nesbit Waddington. This remarkable house has thus remained in the same family for nine generations, covering a period of over 300 years.

Located a few miles from Drogheda on the banks of the Boyne. NGR: O 128767. Open by appointment only and preference given to self-guided groups. Admission to house and gardens: adults IR £3.00. Tel: (041) 38557.

WESTPORT HOUSE

County Mayo

Westport is the largest and most important country house west of the Shannon and the only house by Richard Castle to remain in the possession of the family that built it. Since the late eighteenth century, visitors have marvelled at the building's quality and contents and, above all, its magnificent setting on the edge of Clew Bay, though sadly its fine parkland has been seriously mutilated by development in recent decades.

The house is the work of several architects, although the main mass of the building was designed in 1731 by Richard Castle for John Browne, later the first Earl of Altamont (1709–76). Castle's house incorporated portions of an ancient O'Malley castle that had been acquired and much enlarged by the first Earl's grandfather, Colonel John Browne (1636–1711), a Jacobite who lost his fortune after the Williamite victory at the Boyne. In reduced circumstances, the family moved to Mount Browne outside Westport, but their fortunes prospered again as a result of John Browne's marriage to Anne Gore, sister of the Earl of Arran, in 1729. Two years later the German architect Richard Castle (1695–1751), who later established a highly successful practice in Ireland, began his remodelling of the house. His entrance front remains much as he designed it – a rather austere but attractive nine-bay façade made from beautifully dressed local limestone. Its imposing tripartite doorway, approached by a lengthy flight of steps, has a wide pediment supported by three satyrs' masks and containing the arms of the Earl of Altamont, which must have been added after 1771. Above there are roundels for busts, a three-windowed attic and winged eagles of the family crest at either end of the cornice.

We can see how Westport looked in 1761 from two landscapes by George Moore hanging on the stairs. They show the house in a parkland setting with young plantations, bridges, salmon leaps and the sea coming right up to the house walls. The paintings were commissioned on the completion of John Browne's new park – a massive undertaking that involved not just landscaping and planting trees, but moving the town of Westport from its position around the house to its present location about a mile distant, where a new planned town was created.

Castle's house extended round three sides of an inner court, but between 1776 and 1778 its size was enormously increased when a fourth side was built to the designs of the Cork-born architect Thomas Ivory. This was commissioned by the second Earl of Altamont, whose marriage to an heiress of sugar plantations in Jamaica had made him one of Ireland's richest men. After his death in 1780 the third Earl, John Denis (1756–1809), who was made Marquis of Sligo in 1800, employed James Wyatt to complete the interior. Wyatt's original drawings, dated 1781, are on view in the house. More rooms were added at basement level in 1816 when large terraces were built on either side of the house by the second Marquis, Howe Peter (1788–1845) – remembered for his friendship with George IV and Lord Byron. He brought back to Westport the two columns from the doorway of the Treasury of Atreus at Mycenae when touring Greece in 1812; they remained forgotten in the cellars until discovered by the sixth Marquis who presented them to the British Museum in 1906 on condition that they supply him with the replicas now standing on the south front of the house.

The entrance hall is the only surviving interior by Castle that remains intact. It has a Doric frieze and a magnificent coffered barrel-vaulted ceiling that has been compared to the roof of the temple of Aesculapius at Spoleto. Light pours into the room through a delicately wrought brass lunette above the frieze, though at one time there was also a Venetian window at the west end. The original monumental black marble chimney-piece, a type much favoured by Castle, was considered so oppressive by the family that they replaced it in the 1940s with one brought from Welbeck Abbey in Nottinghamshire. The brilliant Waterford chandelier in this room is one of several in the house, while the parquet floor was laid down in 1857 at the same time as the imperial staircase was installed where the courtyard had been. Approached through arches from the hall, this grand staircase of Sicilian marble was designed for the third Marquis by George Wilkinson to replace two smaller ones on either side. The cantilevered stairs have undercut treads, while the metalwork balustrade, which was made by Skidmore of Coventry, has eagle motifs that were once gilded. In a recess on the half-landing is C. T. Fuller's marble 'Angel of Welcome'; close by are several delightful local landscapes by James O'Connor and a pair of chalk drawings of the children of the second Marquis by F. Wilkin.

The library to the left of the hall replaces one that was designed by Wyatt's son Benjamin in 1819 and subsequently destroyed by fire in 1826. It is a comfortable room whose walls are lined with bookcases stretching to within two feet of the ceiling; to the right of the door is a secret passage said to have been used to hide arms. On the other side of the hall lies the drawing-room, now inexplicably used as a restaurant. This has a frieze of Etruscan figures and a cloud painted ceiling circa 1825, as well as a very fine marble mantelpiece by John Flaxman. The adjoining long gallery, where there is a collection of family portraits, was decorated by James Wyatt but remodelled by his son Benjamin, who removed all the plaster decorations – a great loss if they resembled the plasterwork in the adjacent dining-room.

Although Wyatt never actually came to Ireland, let alone Westport, the delicate Adam-style plasterwork in the dining-room must rank among the best examples of his work. Both walls and ceilings incorporate medallions of classical figures with garlands, bows, festoons and gilded ears of wheat. Originally coloured green and white, the room was repainted grey, blue and gold with touches of red in 1915. The mahogany doors came from the family estates in Jamaica, while the massive sideboards supported by the family eagles were made by Gillow's for the second Marquis. Also on display in this room are Colonel John Browne's dinner service, Waterford glass finger bowls, eighteenth-century silver dish rings and a potato bowl of bog oak and silver that has belonged to the family since the seventeenth century.

There are more family heirlooms in the small dining-room, most notably the flag of the Mayo Legion which was brought to Ireland by General Humbert when he landed in Killala in 1798 with French troops. Elsewhere in the house visitors can see the exceptionally beautiful ceiling by Wyatt above the oak staircase, the Wyatt mantelpiece in the morning room and the Chinese room with its handpainted eighteenth-century wallpaper, which tells the same story as the willow pattern plate.

The property presently belongs to the tenth Marquis of Sligo, whose son and daughter-in-law, the Earl and Countess of Altamont, have opened the house to the public since the 1960s. It is greatly to be regretted that such an important house has had to develop additional attractions such as the zoo in the walled garden in order to meet the outgoings.

Located just outside the town of Westport. NGR: L 987852. Open daily, 17–31 May: 2.00 – 5.00 pm. 1 June to 30 June: 2.00 – 6.00 pm. 1 July to 22 August: 10.30 am – 6.00 pm; Sundays, 2.00 – 6.00 pm. 23 August to 31 August: 2.00 to 6.00 pm. 1 September to 13 September: 2.00 – 5.00 pm. Refreshments available. Toilet facilities. Admission to house: adults IR £4.50; children IR £2.00. Admission to house and zoo: adults IR £5.00; children IR £2.25; family ticket IR £14.50. Tel: (098) 25430/25141.

Clonalis House library

CLONALIS HOUSE

County Roscommon

Front view of Clonalis House

Whatever the great Victorian mansion at Clonalis may
lack in architectural beauty, it certainly gains through
its historical associations with the O'Connor Dons,
descendants of the last High Kings of Ireland whose
possession of these lands can be traced back over 1,500
years. The ruins of the old ancestral seat – an attractive
late seventeenth-century gable-ended house incorporating a medieval castle – can still be seen in the demesne.
This was abandoned in 1880 after the completion of
the present house, a large, rather grim cement-rendered
building of two storeys with a basement and dormered
attic. Its peculiar mixture of Queen Anne Revival and
Victorian Italianate styles is typical of the work of its
designer – Frederick Pepys Cockerell, a young and
popular English architect who died shortly after building work at Clonalis had begun in 1879.

On the lawn in front of the house stands the
inauguration stone of the O'Connors, originally erected
at Rathcroghan, the ancient seat of the High Kings of
Connaught some nine miles distant. The main entrance
to the house is through a balustraded porch set at the
base of a projecting Italianate tower. Entering the
building, visitors will be struck by the height of the hall,
whose modillion ceiling cornice is supported by grace-

ful arches and Ionic columns of pink marble from Mallow. The room has a striking marble bolection chimney-piece, while behind an arcade stands a fine staircase with an oak handrail and pitch-pine balusters. Over the stairs hangs a banner which was carried by Denis O'Connor Don at the coronation of George V in 1911 – the first Irish Gaelic family to be so honoured. Family portraits here include Hugh O'Connor, who founded Tucson in Arizona, and Major Maurice of Ballintober who lost his lands under Cromwell, regained them under Charles II and mortgaged them to raise troops for James II.

A broad arched corridor leads from one side of the hall to the main reception rooms. The first of these to be entered is the large and rather charming drawing-room, which has fine Boulle furniture and some beautifully modelled figures of Meissen, Limoges and Minton porcelain. In the library mahogany bookcases hold over 5,000 books, including the diaries of Charles O'Connor of Belanagare (1710–90), the great historian and antiquary. There are also facsimiles of many early illuminated Irish manuscripts and over 100,000 letters and documents. The room's marble chimney-piece is flanked by niches for turf, as is the chimney in the dining-room where the furniture is mostly Irish Sheraton and the dinner service Mason ironstone. The Roman Catholic chapel contains a number of relics from penal times, including the altar from a secret chapel located in the outbuildings of the old house and a chalice once used by Bishop O'Rourke to celebrate mass, which unscrews into separate pieces for easy concealment.

Some of the most interesting items in the house are found in the billiard room, now converted into a small museum. Here visitors can peruse letters and papers from the family archives, including notes written by such famous personalities as O'Connell, Parnell, Gladstone, Trollope, Napper Tandy, Samuel Johnson and Laurence Stern. However, pride of place in this room is the harp that was once played by Turlough Carolan (1670–1738), the famous blind musician and last of the traditional Irish bards. He often played at Clonalis and once remarked that 'when I am among the O'Connor's, the harp has the old sound in it'.

Located 6½ miles west of Castlerea on the N60. NGR: M 660813. Open daily, 1 June to 12 September: 12.00 – 5.00 pm (closed on Mondays). Afternoon teas available in the tea room. Toilet facilities. Admission: adults IR £2.00; senior citizens IR £1.50; students IR £1.75; children IR £1.00. Tel: (0907) 20014.

STROKESTOWN PARK HOUSE

County Roscommon

Members of the Irish nobility sometimes had rather grand notions, and so it was at Strokestown where the second Lord Hartland laid out a street he wanted wider than the Ringstrasse in Vienna. At one end of this tree-lined mall lies a magnificent Gothic arch that leads to Strokestown Park House, one of Ireland's finest Palladian houses and seat of the Pakenham Mahon family from 1660 to 1979. It now belongs to James Callery of Westward Garage, who purchased the property complete with its contents, saving it from almost certain demolition. He has subsequently carried out a major restoration programme and opened it to the public.

From the front, the house looks enormous with its central block linked by curved quadrants to wings that are prolonged by screen walls with niches and pedimented archways. The main house has seven bays with three storeys over a basement and seems largely to date from 1696 – the date carved on a stone by the front door. The top storey and balustrade were added later, probably around 1740 when the architect Richard Castle built the wings for Thomas Mahon (1701–82), MP for Roscommon for forty-two years. His son Maurice, who became Baron Hartland upon accepting a Union peerage in 1800, made further additions and modifications to the house, including the inlaid mahogany doors, chimney-pieces and cornices as well as the library. In 1819 Lieutenant General Thomas Mahon, second Lord Hartland, employed the architect J. Lynn to carry out some more improvements, such as the addition of the porch and giant pilasters to the front. Except for the gardens, few changes were later carried out at Strokestown and it remained the centre of a vast 30,000-acre estate until the present century.

In contrast to the external grandeur of the house, the interior is quite intimate, with surprisingly small rooms – a product of the early date of much of the building. Early eighteenth-century wood panelling survives in parts of the house, notably in the main staircase hall, but many rooms were redecorated in regency times, such as the dining-room which still has its early nineteenth-century furniture, including a bath-size turf bucket and wonderful pinkish-red damask wallpaper. Regency additions to the house incorporated the study, which also retains its original furnishings, and the smoking room which was converted into a laboratory and photographic dark-room by Henry Pakenham-Mahon, an amateur scientist, in the 1890s. The finest regency addition to the house was the library at the back; originally built as a ball-room with a bowed wall at one end to accommodate musicians, this well-proportioned room has an exuberant and welcoming atmosphere that is remarkable for its unique Chippendale bookcases and for the beauty of its brown-and-gold wallpaper, made especially for these walls in the early nineteenth century.

The old kitchen in the left wing of the house is approached from the dining-room along a curved corridor, past store rooms for kitchen utensils and sporting equipment. Fitted with spits and ovens for baking, roasting and smoking, this kitchen has its original balustraded gallery which crosses the high ceilinged room lengthwise – the only example of its kind to survive in Ireland. Once a familiar feature of many Irish eighteenth-century houses, especially those designed by Richard Castle, these galleries allowed the housekeeper to supervise affairs below – one tradition at Strokestown relates that menus were dropped from the balcony on Monday mornings with the instructions to the cook for the week's meals.

The wing to the right of the central block contains magnificent vaulted stables carried on Tuscan columns – very similar to stables that Castle built for Carton (1739) and Russborough (1741). An underground passage linked these stables to the yard on the north side of the house. The estate office was also housed in this wing – a surprising location, for it meant that the tenantry had to come here rather than to an office in the village to pay their rent. The family's relationship with their tenantry during part of the nineteenth century was not always good. Major Denis Mahon, who succeeded to Strokestown on the death of the third and last Lord Hartland in 1845, was so unpopular a landlord during the famine years that he was shot whilst returning from a meeting of the Roscommon Relief Committee in 1847, apparently on suspicion of having chartered unseaworthy ships to transport emigrants from his estate to America. His successors were much better regarded and his great-granddaughter and last owner, Mrs Olive Hales-Pakenham-Mahon, was a much loved figure in this part of Ireland. She died in 1981, leaving a house filled with the trappings of three centuries of unbroken family occupation.

Located 10 miles west of Longford on the Dublin to Ballina Road (N5). NGR: M 937808. Open 1 June to 12 September: Tuesdays to Sundays and bank holidays, 10.00 am – 5.00 pm. Open to pre-booked tours at other times. Snacks available. Lunch and dinner by prior arrangement. Toilet facilities. Admission: adults IR £3.00; senior citizens IR £2.00; students, children and unemployed IR £1.00; groups of 10+ by enquiry. Tel: (078) 33013.

LISSADELL HOUSE
County Sligo

Few houses have such colourful associations as Lissadell – the large and austere Grecian Revival home of the Gore-Booth family, beautifully situated amidst woods and glades on the north shore of Sligo Bay and immortalised by William Butler Yeats in his poem 'In Memory of Eva Gore-Booth and Con Markiewicz'. As a young man Yeats spent many happy days here with Eva, whom he likened to a gazelle, and Constance, the 'acknowledged beauty of the county'. In later years he fondly remembered the lofty bright rooms of Lissadell with their 'great windows open to the south' and the 'great sitting room as high as a church and all things in good taste'. The old rooms and furnishing remain, their grandeur a little faded now but steeped in remembrance of the many remarkable people who have lived here.

The Gore-Booths stem from an Elizabethan soldier-settler, Sir Paul Gore, ancestor of the Earls of Arran. The Sligo branch first settled at nearby Ardtermon Castle (now restored) but in the eighteenth century moved to a house near the shore at Lissadell. Unfortunately, the damp situation and the danger from high tides was always a problem, so in 1833 Sir Robert

Gore-Booth, fourth Bart (1805–76), commissioned the experienced London architect Francis Goodwin (1784–1835) to design the present house. The conservative tastes of both patron and architect resulted in the adoption of a chaste neo-classical design – the last time this style was used for a large country house in Ireland. The exterior walls of grey Ballysodare limestone incorporate very little ornament apart from corner pilasters and a strong horizontal frieze, while the treatment of the interior is similarly austere, though relieved by a wonderful sensation of bright light and space pervading the rooms.

A *porte cochère* with big oak doors gives access to a broad flight of steps leading up to the front hall – a lofty two-storey room with square Doric columns below and Ionic columns above. Kilkenny marble is used for the floor and also for the magnificent double staircase, notable for its iron balusters decorated with winged birds. Beyond the hall in the core of the house

The drawing-room in Lissadell House

lies an enormous apse-ended gallery sixty-five-feet long, lit by skylights and a clerestory with tall Doric pilasters along one side and freestanding Ionic columns along the other. It was once the music room and retains its original Gothic chamber organ pumped by bellows in the basement. There is also a walnut-topped grand piano, old masters on the walls and souvenirs collected by Sir Robert Gore-Booth on his many travels abroad. His son Sir Henry Gore (1843–1900) was also a great explorer, and in this room stands a model of his yacht *Kara* on which he rescued his friend Leight Smith from

81

the Arctic ice. It is said that Sir Henry's wife Georgina built the artificial lake at Lissadell in the vain hope that he might stay at home and fish in it, but as the harpoons and whale bones in the billiard room testify, Sir Henry was interested in much larger game.

The sequence of hall and gallery leads straight into the library with its 'great windows' in the garden bow, immortalised by Yeats's poem. The massive and rather unusual chimney-piece of this room, like the others in the main reception rooms, shows the influence of Egyptian Revival. The billiard room now displays family memorabilia, including banners presented to Sir Robert Gore-Booth in gratitude for mortgaging the estate during the Famine to help feed the starving thousands of the area – a sacrifice that amounted to a debt of £50,000 over the value of the mortgage and took nearly a century to pay off. The drawing-room has Sir Robert's travelling library of forty-eight leather-bound miniature books, while in the dining-room hang more pictures of the family, including a fine double portrait of the sisters Eva and Constance by Sarah Purser. The pilasters are painted with a remarkable series of life-sized murals that include the gamekeeper, forester and also the butler – the faithful Kilgallon who had accompanied Sir Henry to the Arctic and saved his life by shooting the bear that stands stuffed in the front hall. These icon-like murals are the work of Count Casimir Markievicz, the Polish husband of Constance whom she met at the Paris Art School. Her later exploits are well known; she became involved in the Dublin Lockout of 1913, took part in the 1916 rebellion, was imprisoned and later reprieved from a death sentence, became the first elected female Westminster MP, and later served as Minister of Labour in the first Irish government. She died in 1927, a year after the death of Eva, her equally renowned poet sister.

Some of Constance's own artistic efforts line the walls of the grand staircase along with illuminated addresses presented to her brother, Sir Josslyn Gore-Booth (1869–1944), in recognition of his contribution to the co-operative movement. Sir Josslyn was responsible for establishing the creameries still operating in Sligo and Leitrim; at Lissadell he developed the resources of the estate, planting enormous numbers of trees, building a sawmill, an engineering works and a sewing school and greatly expanding the vegetable and flower gardens. As part of this policy, an important daffodil nursery was built up which later gave rise to many famous cultivars.

After 1944 the government assumed responsibility for the administration of the estate when Sir Josslyn's eldest son was made a ward of the court after a nervous breakdown. During this time the estate went into sharp decline, resulting in the felling of much fine woodland and the compulsory sale in 1968 of 2,600 acres by the Land Commission, leaving only 400 acres around the house. Lissadell now belongs to Sir Josslyn's grandson and, despite its troubles over recent decades, remains here still – a memorial to a family who for generations contributed selflessly to the well-being of Ireland and its people.

Located in Drumcliffe, 20 miles north of Sligo off the Sligo-Bundoran Road. NGR: G 6346. Open daily except Sundays, 1 June – 18 September: 10.30 am – 12.15 pm and 2.00 – 4.15 pm. Tea, coffee and cake available in the old kitchen craft shop. Toilet facilities. Admission: adults IR £2.00; children IR £0.50; groups should book in advance. Tel: (071) 63150.

LISMORE CASTLE
County Waterford

Everyone who has crossed the bridge over the Blackwater River into the town of Lismore will be familiar with this irresistably romantic castle, whose splendid silvery-grey turrets, towers and battlements rise serenely from a cliff above the wooded banks of this most Rhine-like of rivers. While extensively remodelled in the nineteenth century, the walls of Lismore incorporate many earlier buildings with a history stretching back over 1,000 years.

Although the name *Lios Mor* means 'big fort', the castle site was originally occupied by an important monastery and seat of learning established in the early seventh century. It was still an ecclesiastical centre when Henry II stayed here in 1171, and except for a brief period after 1185 when a castle was built here, it served as the episcopal residence of the local bishop. In 1589 Lismore was acquired by Sir Walter Raleigh, who sold the property in 1602 to another famous adventurer, Richard Boyle, later Earl of Cork. Boyle was a man of extraordinary wealth who had arrived in Ireland as a young man in 1588 with only twenty-seven pounds in capital. He never did anything by halves and having decided to make Lismore his principal seat, proceeded to transform it into a magnificent residence with impressive gabled ranges each side of the courtyard. He also made a fortified garden wall with turrets and an outer gatehouse known as the Riding House. The principal apartments were opulently decorated with fretwork plaster ceilings and hangings of tapestry, embroidered silk and velvet. Boyle lived in these apartments with his family and it was here in 1626 that his famous son was born – Robert Boyle, father of modern chemistry. Unfortunately, the castle was sacked by the Confederates in 1645 and although the second Earl made it habitable again, neither he nor his successors, who called themselves by their alternative title of Burlington, were interested in Lismore, preferring to live in England.

The castle was acquired by the Cavandish family in 1753 when the daughter and heiress of the fourth Earl of Cork married the fourth Duke of Devonshire. Their son, the fifth Duke (1748–1811), carried out improvements at Lismore, notably the bridge across the Blackwater in 1775, but it was the sixth Duke (1790–1858), known as the Bachelor Duke, who was responsible for the castle's present appearance. He began transforming the castle into a fashionable 'quasi-feudal ultra-regal fortress' as soon as he succeeded his father in 1811, engaging the architect William Atkinson from 1812 to 1822 to rebuild the castle walls with cut stone shipped over from Derbyshire. The rooms were redesigned with suitably medieval-like Gothic ceilings, the finest undoubtedly in the drawing-room which today contains large tapestries and a magnificent mahogany Irish side-table. This room replaced the old diningroom whose 'great window' is said to have caused James II almost to faint when he saw the dramatic drop to the river below. It was during this period of building that workmen discovered the twelfth-century Lismore Crosier, now in the National Museum, Dublin, and the Book of McCarthy Reagh, popularly known as the Book of Lismore, containing important accounts of the lives of Irish saints.

Lismore was always the Bachelor Duke's favourite residence, but as he grew older his love for the place developed into a passion. In 1850 he engaged his architect Sir Joseph Paxton, the designer of the Crystal Palace, to carry out improvements and additions to the castle on a magnificent scale – so much so, indeed, that the present skyline is largely Paxton's work. At this time J. G. Crace of London, the leading makers of

Gothic Revival furniture, were commissioned to transform the ruined chapel of the old Bishop's Palace into a medieval-style banqueting hall. The great architect A. C. Pugin was commissioned to design the room which he left looking rather appropriately like a church, with a huge perpendicular stained-glass window, choir-stalls and Gothic stenciling on the walls and roof timbers. The chimney-piece, which was exhibited at the Medieval Court of the Great Exhibition of 1851, was also designed by Pugin (and Myers), but was originally intended for Horstead Place in Sussex; it was rejected because it was too elaborate and subsequently bought for Lismore – the Barchard family emblems later replaced with the present inscription *Cead Mille Failte*: a thousand welcomes. Pugin also designed other chimney-pieces and furnishings in the castle and after his death in 1851 Crace continued to supply furnishings in the Puginesque manner.

After the Bachelor Duke's death in 1858 the castle was left more or less as he had redesigned it and has fortunately continued to be loved by his successors who still come here for part of the year.

Located in the town of Lismore. NGR: X 043987. Open by prearrangement to self-guided groups. Lismore Castle is also let out to parties of 4 to 12; for details contact resident agent Mr P. G. Burton. Gardens open daily, 10 May to 10 September, except Saturdays: 1.45 – 4.45 pm. Admission to gardens: adults IR £2.00; children under 16 IR £1.00. Tel: (058) 54424.

Lismore Castle and pleasure grounds

BELVEDERE
County Westmeath

A desire to escape from the formality of country house life during the eighteenth century led to the emergence of small, comfortable holiday retreats known as villas. Undoubtedly the best example of such a building in Ireland is Belvedere – an exquisite house with an unusual elongated plan set in a fine landscape park overlooking Lough Ennell. Belvedere was built around 1742 to a design by Richard Castle, probably as a fishing pavilion, for Robert Rochfort, Lord Belfield, whose seat at Gaulston lay five miles away. Like other villas of the period, the building was distinguished from ordinary houses of the same size by the exceptionally high quality of its design and construction, most notably its superb joinery and brilliant plasterwork. But the very strange and terrible events that preceded its construction ensured that Belvedere was never really used as a villa, but rather became a country house in its own right.

Belvedere had hardly been completed in 1743 when a great scandal broke out surrounding its builder, Robert Rochfort, and his wife Mary Molesworth. She was only sixteen when she married Robert in 1736, but at the time the match seemed highly suitable; he was intelligent, handsome and one of the country's richest young men, she was the pretty and well-connected daughter of the third Viscount Molesworth. They settled at Gaulston and all seemed well until 1743 when Robert, now Baron Belfield, was informed that his wife had committed adultery with his young brother Arthur, then living near Gaulston at Belfield. Robert, evidently a hot-tempered and self-centred individual, at once removed to his newly completed house at Belvedere, incarcerated his wife at Gaulston and plotted revenge against his brother, who fled to England. For thirty-one years his wife remained confined at Gaulston with only servants to keep her company. Once in 1756 she managed to escape, but her father refused her entry into his house and within twenty-four hours she was back in Gaulston. Henceforth her movements were further restricted and she was no longer allowed visits by her children. It is said that she used to walk up and down the gallery at Gaulston gazing at the portraits 'as if conversing with them'. After her husband's death in 1774 she was released by her son, who was horrified to find that she had acquired a 'wild, scared, unearthly look, whilst the tones of her voice, which hardly exceeded a whisper, were harsh, agitated and uneven'. As for the unfortunate Arthur, he made the mistake of returning to Ireland in 1759 and was sued for adultery by his unrelenting brother, now Earl of Belvedere. Fined £20,000 in damages, he spent the rest of his life in the Marshalsea, the debtor's jail in Dublin.

Lord Belvedere's treatment of his wife makes gripping reading, but it is also an indictment of eighteenth-century social attitudes. What is so striking is that his behaviour did his reputation no harm at all. At Belvedere he lived an extravagant lifestyle, entertained a great deal and rose through the social ranks to become Earl of Belvedere in 1756 and Master General of the Irish army in 1764.

Although its rooms are now empty, Belvedere remains much as it was in the Earl's time. A solid grey limestone house of two stories over a basement with a long front and curved end bows, it is probably the earliest bow-ended house in the country. Above the Venetian windows on the front there were formerly Diocletian or semi-circular openings, but unfortunately these were changed to their present shape in the nineteenth century. The Venetian and the bow windows provided light for the drawing-room and dining-room at either end of the house and between them are two small rooms (now united as one), a corridor and a handsome wooden staircase in a projection at the back of the building. Both the end rooms are grand but not large, with unusual chamfered corners and very high-quality joinery – their doors, windows and wainscotting all remain unpainted. The drawing-room chimney-piece is a Victorian addition, but other fireplaces and overmantels are original to the house, including a fine example in the east bedroom, probably Lord Belvedere's room.

The delicate rococo plasterwork ceilings are the real glory of Belvedere's interior. Framed by rich cornices, these ceilings are notable for their lively quality and freedom of movement. The drawing-room ceiling has scrollwork enclosing medallions of Juno, Minerva and Venus, while that in the dining-room is rather bolder, with clusters of fruit and flowers and four puffing cherubs emerging from clouds in the centre. In the hall the plasterwork is in much lower relief and is supposed to represent the night, with an owl, a flaming torch, stars and more swirling clouds. The name of the plasterer is unknown, but it has been noted that the work closely resembles ceilings formerly at Mespil House outside Dublin; these are believed to have been the work of the Frenchman Bartholomew Cramillion, who is known to have made the splendid rococo ceiling in the Rotunda Hospital Chapel in 1755.

The small park that Lord Belvedere created around his villa is just as fine as the house itself and was the envy of all visitors, not least John Wesley who in 1767 remarked that 'one would scarce think it possible to have such a variety of beauties in so small a compass'. One of the attractions was an enormous sham Gothick ruin, which Lord Belvedere in typical fashion built to block out the view of Rochfort House (later known as Tudenham), the home of another of his brothers with whom he had quarrelled. Yet despite his violent and cruel temperament, the Earl was certainly a man of taste and the Gothick arch he had built at the other end of the park is one of the most endearing follies in Ireland.

Following the death of the 'Wicked Earl' (as he was later known) in 1774, the house was inherited by his son, the second Earl, who sold Gaulston and continued to live at Belvedere where he added a small wing to the back. Although his father had left him 'very embarrassed in his circumstances' he managed to revive the family fortunes sufficiently to build a magnificent town residence – now the home of a famous Dublin school. He died without heirs in 1814 and the property was inherited by his sister, the Countess of Lanesborough, and later passed in 1826 to her great-grandson, Charles Brinsely Marley, who lived at Belvedere until his death in 1912. Marley laid out the Italianate terraces in front of the house and assembled a remarkable collection of pictures and *objets d'art* which was given to Cambridge University upon his death, forming the core of the Fitzwilliam Museum. The residue of this collection together with the house and estate were left to his cousin Lieutenant Colonel C. K. Howard-Bury, leader of the 1921 Mount Everest expedition, who after his death in 1963 bequested it to Rex Beaumont. The contents were auctioned by Christie's in 1980 – a catastrophic loss for any such house. However, the interior of Belvedere is so fine that it still retains its soul, empty as the rooms may be.

Located 4 miles from Mullingar on the Tullamore Road. NGR: N 420477. Open daily, 1 April to 30 October: 12.00 – 6.00 pm. Refreshments available on Sundays. Toilet facilities. Admission: adults IR £1.00; children IR £0.50. Tel: (044) 42820.

TULLYNALLY CASTLE

County Westmeath

During the early nineteenth century, a craze for building sham castles spread across Ireland with remarkable speed, undoubtedly provoked by a sense of unease in the aftermath of the 1798 rebellion. Security was certainly a factor in Johnson's 1801 to 1806 remodelling of Tullynally, otherwise known as Pakenham Hall, where practical defensive features such as a portcullis entrance were included in addition to romantic looking battlements and turrets. Later enlargements during the 1820s and 1830s were also fashioned in the castle style and made Tullynally into one of the largest castellated houses in Ireland – so vast, indeed, that it has been compared to a small fortified town.

Masonry walls ten-feet thick are all that remain of the castle that originally stood here in 1655 when Tullynally was purchased by Henry Pakenham, ancestor of the Earls of Longford. By the 1730s this stronghold had been transformed into a grand two-storey house surrounded by extensive formal gardens with canals. Traces of panelling and a few chimney-pieces still survive from this building, which was remodelled in 1780 as a five-bay three-storey classical block to the designs of Graham Myers, the architect of Trinity College. It was this building which Francis Johnson, the outstanding architect of his generation in Ireland, was commissioned in 1801 to gothicise for the second Earl of Longford. Johnson designed battlements and label mouldings over the windows, but as work progressed it was felt this treatment was too tame, so between 1805 and 1806 more dramatic features were added, notably round corner turrets and a portcullis entrance, transforming the house with characteristic Irish nomenclature from Pakenham Hall House to Pakenham Hall Castle.

Additions to Johnson's work were made by the second Earl in the early 1820s when James Shiel added a bow on the east garden front and redesigned the entrance hall. More substantial additions followed between 1839 and 1846 when Richard Morrison, that other stalwart of the Irish architectural scene, was employed by the Dowager Countess to bring the house up to improved Victorian standards of convenience. Under Morrison's direction the main house and Johnson's stable court were linked by two parallel wings, both of which were elaborately castellated and faced externally with grey limestone. Following the fashion recently made popular by the great Scottish architect William Burn, one of the new wings contained a private apartment for the family, while the other on the east side of the courtyard contained larger and more exactly differentiated servants' quarters with elaborate laundries and a splendid kitchen. After the third Earl's death in 1860 his brother succeeded to the title and property and proceeded to modernise the castle with all the latest equipment for supplying water, heat and lighting. Except for a water tower erected in the stable court by the Dublin architect J. Rawson Carroll in the 1860s, these modifications did not involve altering the fabric of the building, which has remained remarkably unchanged to the present day.

Visitors entering the castle will first arrive in the great hall – an enormous room forty-feet square and thirty-feet high with no gallery to take away from its impressive sense of space. A central-heating system was designed for this room by Richard Lovell Edgeworth, who earlier in 1794 had fitted up the first semaphore telegraph system in Ireland between Edgeworthstown and Pakenham Hall, a distance of twelve miles. In a letter written in December 1807, his daughter Maria Edgeworth, a frequent visitor to Pakenham Hall, wrote that 'the immense hall is so well-warmed by hot air that the children play in it from morning to night. Lord L. seemed to take great pleasure in repeating twenty times that he was to thank Mr. Edgeworth for this.' Edgeworth's heating system was, in fact, so effective that when Shiel remodelled the hall in 1820 he replaced one of the two fireplaces with a built-in organ that visitors can see. James Shiel was also responsible for the Gothic vaulting of the ceiling, the Gothic niches containing the family crests, the high wood panelling around the base of the walls and the massive cast-iron Gothic fireplace. Other features of the room include a number of attractive early nineteenth-century drawings of the castle, a collection of old weapons, family portraits and an Irish elk's head dug up out of a bog – once a familiar feature of Irish country house halls.

A door opposite the main entrance across the hall leads into the dining-room, which was remodelled by Shiel into an octagon that extends into a canted bay window facing east. It has oak panelling similar to the hall (once painted green), wallpaper designed by Pugin for the House of Lords and a ceiling of plaster half-vaults. Family portraits hang on the walls and the furniture is mostly flamboyant Irish Chippendale, while the table has Mason ironstone china and Irish champagne glasses.

Another door from the hall leads into the drawing-room which retains its appearance from Johnson's remodelling of the house, including a decorated ceiling in the geometric manner. This is a pleasant room with canvases of sea battles, a Chinese cabinet handpainted by an Irishman and a dinner service donated to Admiral Sir Thomas Pakenham by grateful German merchants rescued from pirates. The adjacent library, which also has magnificent views over rolling parkland, is a spacious and comfortable room; oak bookcases tower from floor to ceiling and a delightful alcove stands in one corner. Over the mantelpiece is a portrait of the second Earl's brother, Sir Edward Pakenham, a Peninsular War general who later lost his life at the Battle of New Orleans in the War of 1812. The distinguished military past of the Pakenhams has been replaced this century by an equally distinguished literary tradition. Family members include the present Earl of Longford, who has written numerous books including the lives of Nixon and de Valera; his wife Elizabeth, who has written important biographies of the Duke of Wellington and Queen Victoria; their son Thomas Pakenham, author of highly acclaimed accounts of the 1798 rebellion, the South African War and the colonial struggle for Africa; his sister Antonia Fraser, another distinguished biographer, and Rachel Billington, a novelist.

One of the most fascinating features of Tullynally Castle is surely the rooms belowstairs. Visitors can tour the splendid kitchen with its great ovens, a great pestle and mortar, an early ice chest and a dresser with gleaming brassware probably bought for the kitchen when it was built in the 1840s. Sadly, because this kitchen remained in continuous use its huge 1875 range was replaced by an Aga in the 1940s. Other rooms of special interest include the Victorian laundries, which remain largely as they were after being remodelled between 1863 and 1864 by the fourth Earl. Here the inquisitive will find a wash house with lead-lined sinks and a giant mangle with a heavy roller used for sheets, an ironing room (now used as a tea room) and a drying-room fitted up with vertical racks on rails that could be pulled in and out of a heated chamber. Some of the drying, however, had to be done in an open-air drying-yard beyond the stables; this was approached by a sunken passage allowing the laundry maids (who were apt to be pretty) to carry the washing to the yard without having to meet any of the grooms on the way.

Located 1 mile outside of Castlepollard on the Granard Road, 13 miles from Mullingar. NGR: N 445705. Open daily, 15 July to 15 August: 2.00 – 6.00 pm. Open to groups at other times by written appointment. The gardens are open daily from June to September: 10.00 am – 6.00 pm. Toilet facilities. Admission to castle: adults IR £1.50; senior citizens and children IR £0.50. Admission to castle and gardens: adults IR £3.50; senior citizens and children IR £1.50. Tel: (044) 61159/61289.

RUSSBOROUGH

County Wicklow

Irish country houses are generally distinguished by their architecture rather than their contents, but Russborough is a striking exception to this rule. Not only does this magnificent Palladian mansion boast lavish plasterwork, splendid chimney-pieces and superb joinery, but it also contains the world-famous Beit collection of pictures, furniture and *objets d'art*. It can justifiably be said that Russborough, with its superb landscape setting, is indeed a temple of the arts – a place of rare quality and beauty.

The house was commissioned by Joseph Lesson, later the first Earl of Milltown (1705–83), after inheriting the wealth of his father, an opulent Dublin brewer. Completion of the building which began in 1741 took over ten years so that its designer, Richard Castle (1690–1751), never lived to see the final stages that were carried out by his associate Francis Bindon. The house is built of local silver-grey granite with wonderfully crisp detail and has an entrance front that extends to 700 feet, the longest in Ireland. The centre block of seven bays and two stories over a basement is relatively small, but is extended via colonnaded quadrant wings to seven-bay, two-storey pavilions. Further out stretch high plain walls, each broken by a centrally placed rusticated arch terminating in one-storey pavilions associated with the kitchen and stableyards. Fortune has smiled kindly upon Russborough for it has remained free of subsequent alterations, with most of Castle's original features surviving intact.

Ascending the broad flight of granite steps guarded by a pair of carved lions, the visitor enters the front hall – a well-proportioned room with a floor of polished oak and an ornate but severe compartmental ceiling with Doric frieze quite similar to the one Castle designed for Leinster House. The monumental chimney-piece is of black Kilkenny marble, much favoured by Castle for entrance halls, while above it hangs a striking painting by Oudry of 'Indian Black-buck with Pointers and Still Life', dated 1745. Five doors with magnificently carved architraves of West Indian mahogany lead to the major reception rooms: the saloon, the drawing-room, the dining-room, the tapestry room and the grand staircase.

Undoubtedly the finest room in the house is the saloon, which occupies the three central bays of the north front. It has a coved ceiling with rococo plaster-work incorporating flowers, garlands, swags and putti, which on stylistic grounds can be attributed to the Francini brothers of Italy. The walls are covered with a crimson cut Genoese velvet dating from around 1840 – an ideal background for paintings which include the principal Dutch and Flemish pictures in the Beit collection. The room also has Louis XVI furniture in Gobelins tapestry signed by Pluvinet, a pair of Japanese lacquer cabinets from Harewood House and a chimney-piece identical to one at Uppark in Sussex, which must be the work of Thomas Carter (the younger) of London. A striking feature of the room is the inlaid sprung mahogany floor with a central star in satinwood. This was covered with a green baize drugget when the house was occupied by rebels during the 1798 rebellion. The potential of the drugget for making four fine flags was considered but rejected by the rebels, lest 'their brogues might ruin his lordship's floor'. The rebels, in fact, did virtually no damage to the house during their stay, although the government forces who occupied the building afterwards were considerably less sympathetic. It is said that the troops only left in 1801 after a furious Lord Milltown challenged Lord Tyrawley to a duel 'with underbusses and slugs in a sawpit'.

Flanking the saloon along the north front is the music room and the library, formerly the dining-room, both framed by ebullient rococo ceilings that were probably also the work of the Francini brothers. The coffered and richly decorated barrel-vaulted ceiling of the tapestry room, to the south of the music room, is by a less experienced artist, though the room is no less impressive than the others and contains an English state bed made in London in 1795 and two Soho tapestries of Moghul subjects by Vanderbank. Infused with a restless energy the plasterwork in the adjacent drawing-room spills onto the walls, where fantastic plaster frames surround the four oval marine scenes by Vernet representing morning, noon, evening and night. Although part of the patrimony of the house, these pictures were sold in 1926 and only after a determined search were recovered forty-three years later by Sir Alfred Beit. Beyond lies the boudoir – a charming little panelled apartment with a Bossi chimney-piece dating around 1780. From here visitors pass into the tapestry-hung corridor leading to the pavilion, formerly the bachelor's quarters. The dining-room, formerly the library, on the opposite side of the hall has a monumental Irish chimney-piece of mottled grey Sicilian marble. The walls are ornamented by a series of six Murillo paintings acquired by Alfred Beit from Lord Dudley in 1895. Five of these pictures were purchased in 1867 at the Salamanca sale in Paris, while the sixth was later acquired by Dudley from the Vatican Museum in exchange for a Fra Angelico and a Bonifazio.

No one who visits Russborough is likely to forget the staircase with its extraordinary riot of exuberant plasterwork; there is nothing quite like it anywhere else in the British Isles. In later years the decorator Mr Sibthorpe is reported to have remarked that it represented 'the ravings of a maniac', adding that he was 'afraid the madman was Irish'.

On the death of the sixth Earl of Milltown in 1890, Russborough passed to his widow and later to his nephew before being sold out of the family in 1931. Fortunately, most of its famous art collection assembled by the first Earl remained in Ireland when the sixth Earl's widow bequeathed it to the National Gallery of Ireland in 1902 – a bequest so important that a new wing was built to contain it. Russborough was not devoid of art treasures for long, however; the property was acquired by Sir Alfred Beit in 1951 as the setting for one of the world's most outstanding private art collections. Dominated by Dutch, Flemish and Spanish masterpieces, this collection was largely formed by Alfred Beit (1853–1906), a co-founder with Cecil Rhodes of the De Beers Diamond Mining Company in South Africa. The house and its collection have now been given to a foundation and are open to the public, while the Beits have moved into one of the wings. It is extremely sad that the Beits' remarkable generosity to the Irish people was rewarded in 1986 by a robbery of some of the finest pictures in the house. It must earnestly be hoped that these will all be recovered and returned to their rightful place in this wonderful house.

Located 2½ miles south west of Blessington. NGR: N 957100. Open daily during Easter, and Sundays and bank holidays in April, May, September and October: 10.30 am – 5.30 pm. Open daily during June to August: 10.30 am – 5.30 pm. Visits outside advertised hours may be pre-arranged. Tea room. Toilet facilities. Collection of miniature steam locomotives in basement. Guided tours available. Admission: adults IR £2.50; senior citizens and students IR £1.50; children IR £1.00; children under 12 IR £0.50. Reductions for pre-booked groups. There is an additional fee of IR £1.00 for visits to the upstairs rooms. Tel: (045) 65239.

The blue bedroom at Springhill

SUPPLEMENTARY
COUNTRY HOUSES

Cratloe Woods House, Co. Clare. 5 miles NW of Limerick. Gable-ended 17th-century longhouse. A seat of a branch of the O'Briens who claim ancestry from Brien Boru. Open 1 June–mid September: Mon–Sat, 2.00–6.00 pm. IR £2.00; senior citizens/students IR £1.50; children IR £1.00. Tel: (061) 327028.

Blarney House, Blarney, Co. Cork. Scottish baronial mansion (1874) in ashlar with turrets, bartizans and conical roof. Fine interior includes Jacobean-style oak staircase. Famous medieval castle and 18th-century folly 'Rock Close', 200 yards distant within park. House and gardens open 1 June–mid September: Mon–Sat, 12.00–6.00 pm. IR £2.50; senior citizens/students IR £1.50; children IR £1.00. Tel: (021) 385252.

Myrtle Grove, Youghal, Co. Cork. Protected by ancient town walls, this is the only example of an unfortified Tudor manor house to survive in Ireland. Panelling and carved overmantel of great chamber date back to when the house was the Irish home of Sir Walter Raleigh. Guided tours: June, 3.00 & 4.30 pm; July–August, 11.45 am, 3.00 pm & 4.30 pm. Bookings for organised groups at other times by prior arrangement: 1 May–30 September. IR £3.00; senior citizens/students/children IR £2.00. Tel: (024) 92274.

Riverstown House, Glanmire, Co. Cork. Early 17th-century house, enlarged and remodelled in 1730s when it was given very fine plasterwork by the Francini brothers. Open May–August: Thurs–Sat, 2.00–6.00 pm; other times by appointment. IR £2.00. Tel: (021) 821205.

Glenveagh Castle, Churchill, Co. Donegal. Romantically located baronial castle, built in 1870 for Adair family. From 1939 to 1973 was the home of the late Henry McIlhenny whose famed art collection still largely remains in the castle. Open Easter–31 October: 10.30 am–6.30 pm. Sundays in June—August: 10.00 am–7.30 pm. IR £1.50 to castle & gardens; children IR £0.60. Tel: (074) 37088.

Slane Castle, Slane, Co. Meath. Gothic revival castle in dramatic setting overlooking River Boyne. Due to extensive damage by fire, castle and grounds are closed; will re-open when restoration is completed.

Country House Ruins Accessible to the Public:

Mount Shannon, Castleconnell, Co. Clare. Neo-classical mansion of Earls of Clare, once magnificently furnished. Burnt 1922. Dramatic ruins include a *porte cochère*.

Downhill, Castlerock, Co. L'Derry. Palace built 1771–87 on bare cliff-top by Frederick Hervey, Bishop of Derry & Earl of Bristol. Ruin made safe by National Trust in 1980s.

Thomastown Castle, Golden, Co. Tipperary. Amazing ruins of late 17th-century mansion, enlarged and remodelled in the castle style by Richard Morrison for Mathew family in 1812.